Growing with Community Gardening

Mary Lee Coe

Illustrations by John Winthrop Fowler

The Countryman Press
Taftsville, Vermont

Illustrations © 1978 by John Winthrop Fowler

Printed in the United States of America
by Northlight Studio Press, Barre, Vermont

Library of Congress Cataloging in Publication Data

Coe, Mary Lee.
  Growing with community gardening.

  Bibliography: p.
  Includes index.
  1. Community gardens. 2. Community gardens—United States. I. Title. II. Title: Community gardening.
SB457.3.C63   301.34   78-1454
ISBN 0-914378-36-8
ISBN 0-914378-22-8 pbk.

Contents

Preface

Mary Lee Coe's book *Growing With Community Gardening* deserves to be read because it is a complete guide to community gardening. Not only is it concerned with plants and how to grow them but perhaps even more important, it is concerned with the people who grow their vegetables and flowers, often in harsh urban sites. It is Ms. Coe's sensitivity to the human aspect of gardening that distinguishes this book from most other "how to" horticultural books. She examines the human aspect of community gardening; who gardens, why they garden, what benefits are gained, and the kinds of personal commitment required to make these projects successful.

The book is a careful guide to establishing successful community gardens. Through samples of programs in several cities, she analyzes the qualities that determine success or frustration. The book is replete with step by step instructions for setting up community gardens, illustrated with diagrams, planting charts and the knowhow that can make such programs a success.

It is a book for people who wish to understand the subtle personal qualities that make gardening more than a horticultural experience. It should be of immense help to anyone wishing to establish a community gardening program.

Charles A. Lewis, Horticulturist
Lisle, Illinois

Introduction

What Is Community Gardening?

In the spring of 1971, I moved to land I had recently purchased in a newly-formed intentional community of 180 uncultivated acres of woods and marshland. One of our first resolutions was to make a community garden, more for the sense of unity we were certain derived from such a project than for the winter's mountain of wholesome produce we imagined looming in our non-existent root cellars.

So instead of building our houses, we came from our separate campsites to meet in a small pocket of second growth, and with a rented bulldozer spent the black-flied month of May clearing brush and heaving rocks. We ended up with a multi-sloped site requiring terracing, which we did by digging notches in the hillsides and filling them with the standing dead spruce growing along the edge of the nearby marsh. The final effect was surprisingly oriental and we got so carried away with the aesthetics, certain of a near future of arched stone bridges and delicate teahouses, that we cheerfully under-fertilized and neglected to fence in our finished plot.

Filled with the hubris and blind optimism of fledgling homesteaders, we felt that camping on a ledge overlooking the valley would keep all hungry critters away. The sight of terrace upon terrace of seeds sprouting and seedlings taking hold made us so heady with success that we were dumbstruck the morning after the woodchuck made its first fatal night visit. In fact, the coming of the woodchuck began a maturing process of several years that finally came to fruition in a second community garden. But more of that later.

The woodchuck had stripped all the pods off the Chinese snow peas and lopped all seedlings down to the ground. There was *nothing* left. All we could do was beat a bewildered retreat back to our campsites to salvage what growing season was left us in our own separate gardens and to try to extract a lesson from the demise of our precious would-be tea garden.

Our first instinct was to blame the guy who had persuaded us that the very idea of fencing was just "negative tripping." Our subsequent working and mulling in separate gardens showed us what all our idealistic back-to-the-land theory couldn't: that in successful gardening, one head is better than two, three or ten, unless there is perfect community. Being a new community of urban refugees rebelling against structure, we hadn't even the benefit of the natural pecking order achieved in ordinary nuclear families; we had neither the hierarchy nor the confidence that

1

comes from the certainty of one's place in an order. Thus we were unable to veto the fence vetoer. There were too many opinions with no established basis of discrimination.

This lack of structure has plagued communal gardens from their beginnings in the back-to-the-land movement of the late 1960's and early 1970's. "Communal" is the designation I have given to a single plot garden planned and worked by a group, to distinguish this effort from the alternative that developed over the last few years, the community garden. The most common complaint I encountered from former communal gardeners was that there was no way of enforcing responsibility, that certain individuals just couldn't be relied upon to do their share of the weeding and other unpalatable chores, to the jeopardy of the entire garden. The most successful communal gardens I have found are at institutions such as schools or monasteries with a fairly stable population and a preexisting hierarchy and structure that are adhered to upon entrance. Intentional communities lack the essential authority to delegate responsibility effectively.

The alternative to the communal way is the community garden, which grew into a national phenomenon by 1975 as a result of inflation and high food costs. Community gardens are individual plots on an area privately owned and leased or loaned to the gardeners or on public property. They most often provide garden space for apartment and city dwellers who have no space of their own. The basic working unit is the family, thus the necessary pecking order has long since been established and there is enough unity, if not harmony, to get the job done. In 1976, fifty-one percent of all U.S. families had vegetable gardens and ten percent of these were community gardens.[1]

There are community gardens in all fifty states, some of them assisted or sponsored by the U.S. Department of the Interior's Bureau of Outdoor Recreation (hereafter referred to as the BOR) and the U.S. Department of Agriculture's Cooperative Extension Services. The most exciting result of this nationwide community garden drive is that millions of people who don't otherwise get the opportunity are being exposed to the joys and wisdom of gardening and sound nutritional practices. Most of the BOR gardens have courses in conjunction with the program on nutrition, organics, gardening skills, and freezing and canning techniques.[2]

The ideal garden site suggested by the BOR would be fitted with portable toilets, picnic tables, children's playgrounds, and volley-ball courts, to provide an infectious family recreation experience at minimal cost for an entire growing season. The balance of work and play provided by such a site produces a most effective

1. Gallup Organization, Princeton, N.J., Survey conducted for Gardens For All, Inc., Bulletin of Gardens For All: *News About Community Gardening—1976*, (Jan. 15, 1976), p. 1.
2. Susan York Drake and Roberta L. Lawrence, *Recreational Community Gardening*, U.S. Dep't. of Interior, Bureau of Outdoor Recreation Booklet.

learning experience that brings families back year after year. Nearly half the community gardens, forty-eight percent, around the country in existence since 1974 expanded in 1975 and planned to expand in 1976.[3]

Community gardening has grown into a sociological phenomenon that can transform society from the roots.

Why Community Gardening?

The coming of the woodchuck to our first communal garden was only the beginning of a series of similar lessons that taught me with painful finality that long hair, gentle manners, the desire to live simply, and even shared reverence for nature do not a community make. Nor even a garden. There are many material details that shared values don't anticipate, specifics that need to be lived through once before the resulting differences can be avoided in later development. Our community had been founded on the kind of idealism that was irresistible to me at the time I bought in: that we are all brothers and sisters, so why shouldn't we live as a loving, supportive family combining the best of communalism through common gardening, and individualism through private ownership of separate homesites.

Making requirements for membership to this fondly imagined family was one of those material details that we weren't up to wrestling with before the consequences. We waived responsibility by declaring that the land would choose its people. Escape from our urban and suburban puritan heritage of straight thinking had been a large reason why most of us had come "back to the land" in the first place, and in our reactive emphasis on spontaneity, "vibes," and intuitive flashes, we were almost ethically bound not to make judgments about prospective buyers. Thus the facile assumption that the land would choose its people was an easy solution to any problems we might have foreseen if we hadn't dumped our intellectual responsibility to discriminate.

Needless to say, the conglomeration of gardeners that resulted from our summer's flight from reason made a horticultural Tower of Babel that, when the woodchuck brought it down, sent us careening off to privacy with a vengeance in our separate homestead gardens. Three years elapsed before we ventured out to try a second communal garden. What the land taught us in that interim made our second attempt a success, with high yields and a camaraderie that made our worktimes pure pleasure.

Our success was a result not only of three years of learning and developing proper gardening techniques but also of the profound spiritual change that gardening wrought in us, which I feel is gardening's most important harvest. I discovered

3. Gardens For All, Inc., op. cit., p. 1.

evidence of this change that first summer when I made my own private garden; with my hands in the soil and the certainty that I was working *with* nature came a feeling of serenity that I had never felt before. This feeling of peace, of my mind naturally clearing of the daily debris of plans, projections, and speculations, pervaded my consciousness each time I worked my small plot, until I began to use the garden experience as daily meditation.

Experts in the human potential movement believe that the desire to alter consciousness every so often is an innate human drive corresponding to the drive for sex or food. One claims that today's widespread use of drugs is a symptom of this unconscious urge to go from our normal waking state to a different psychic level.[4] A hundred years ago, when a far greater proportion of people lived in the country and spent their days underscoring the direct relationship between human life and the soil, there was more exposure to the natural conditions that foster mystical experience. Meditation is a healthier way to alter consciousness than drugs, and working in the garden is a short-cut to slowing down and letting one's consciousness find its own unique access to new levels. A group gardening experience, if there is structure and unity, can heighten this mind expansion, much as a stoned individual or group can effect a "contact high" on a newcomer.

Rachel Kaplan, a psychologist at the University of Michigan, made a landmark study of the psychological benefits of nature experiences and elaborates on the mind-expanding effect of gardening, an effect she explains as *fascination:*

> ...Such feelings evoke memories of William James' (1892) descriptions of "involuntary attention." While voluntary attention requires effort and is difficult to sustain, involuntary attention is effortless. If nature in general and gardening in particular can lead to involuntary attention, this has several obvious benefits. First, it provides a rest from the effort otherwise required for attention. Second, since attention by definition excludes competing thoughts, a rest is provided from whatever worries or cares of the day might otherwise be uppermost in a person's mind. This hypothesized benefit, centering on fascination, is clearly distinct from the more prosaic but still powerful benefit of harvesting one's own food, of participating in a basic survival process.[5]

She concludes her study with the reasons gardening enhances fascination:

> It is in retrospect hardly surprising that gardening emerges as a powerful source of fascination. It appears to possess a great many properties that would tend to enhance fascination. First, it calls on the basic informational processes that humans do so well and presumably care so deeply about. It not only permits, but actually invites recognition, prediction, control, and evaluation (S. Kaplan, 1972). It does this by both providing

4. Andrew Weil, *The Natural Mind,* (Boston, Houghton Mifflin Co., 1973), p. 19.

5. Rachel Kaplan, "Some Psychological Benefits of Gardening." *Environment and Behavior,* Vol. 5, No. 2, (June 1973) p. 146.

knowledge and requiring it. It is a setting that allows of order, but that order is deeply embedded in uncertainty and change. Thus, it challenges the human-information-processing capability, and to the extent that the challenge is met, both reward and more challenge are forthcoming. Second, it is a nature-based activity, and nature per se has been shown to be the object of preference to a striking degree....(Kaplan et al., 1972).

Finally, both of these virtues, the informational and the natural, are in the garden setting concentrated and intensified. The garden is a miniature, a slice of nature compressed in time. Rarely is so broad a spectrum of nature and natural processes found in so little area. Rarely are so much nature-based action and so full a view of the life cycle so vividly visible and so rapidly completed.[6]

Thus by the time we got to our second communal garden, the fascination and sheer pleasure associated with being in the garden pervaded the project, making everyone considerably more amenable to structure and generally more affectionate so that unity was easier to attain. And we got high on gardening *together*. However, we found that this euphoria still didn't circumvent the most common blight of communal gardens: that the same few people performed all the most unpalatable tasks. The Ecology Center's organic garden in Ann Arbor, Michigan, is one of the few successful communal efforts that did not have a common ideological or institutional base. Its success is based on a strict commitment (a signed contract at the beginning of the growing season) to six gardening principles, reviewed in detail in the chapter on organization, which form a tight structure. Such tightness is the only way to ensure equal participation and responsibility.

Besides providing a climate conducive to meditation, relaxation, and fascination, gardening—and particularly group gardening because of the pooling of resources—can yield a careful gardener over $250 worth of fresh vegetables each year.[7] And these vegetables, if grown organically, taste superbly different from supermarket produce and are more nutritious. Chromatographic analysis by practitioners of the biodynamic method, an early school of organic gardening founded by the Austrian philosopher Rudolf Steiner, show that vegetables grown by organics are brimming with vitamins and minerals compared to supermarket specimens. Analyses run over several years at a biodynamic laboratory in Jarna, Sweden, have shown that potatoes grown by the biodynamic method have a higher vitamin content and keep fresh longer than those grown with commercial fertilizers.[8]

The psychological and ecological need for each of us to turn to the production of such a nutritious alternative to the supermarket is increasingly vital as prices soar and the planet's resources shrink. Dr. W.H. Newsome of Canada's Department

6. Ibid., p. 160.

7. Gardens For All, Inc., op. cit., p. 2.

8. R. Nilsson, "The Big Organic Farm and the Man Who Made It Work." *Organic Gardening and Farming,* Vol. 19, No. 11 (November, 1972), p. 46.

of National Health and Welfare has found ETU residues (ethylene Thiourea, a breakdown product of a fungicide sprayed on many food crops) in measurable levels in apples and spinach purchased in U.S. and Canadian grocery stores as of 1972. ETU is a health hazard, having caused cancer in test animals. In the face of growing evidence of pesticide residues in our drinking water and their occasional storage in the human body,[10] we can no longer afford to blindly buy vegetables at the supermarket where they are selected for eye appeal and the firmness to withstand high-speed harvesting and long-distance hauling (lettuce-harvesting machines have "feeler" mechanisms which reject too-tender heads).[11] On the ramifications of the production techniques of such superfarming, Ralph S. Widrig, a Canadian chemist and organic gardener, has this to say in *Sea Breezes and Vegetable Gardening:*

> ...more than 250 new chemical compounds have been devised and marketed that were intended to kill troublesome insects, or "pests."...They have killed insects both good and bad... killed fish in our rivers and streams, birds and wildlife in our forests, and have contaminated the soils of vast areas of fertile farmland... the net result of this senseless performance has, in many cases, produced strains of the troublesome insects that have emerged stronger and more numerous than ever - and immune to the particular new poison. And so today many companies are advertising 'improved, multiple-action pesticides' in a frantic effort to overcome the forces of natural evolution which brought about this immunity. These new 'multi-action' or 'broad-spectrum' pesticides are mixtures of poisons that are many times more toxic than each constituent would be if used alone.
>
> Almost all of these new chemical insecticides are very definitely poisonous to human beings, and the mixtures are even more lethal. This has been difficult to believe when perusing the 'garden-aid' counter of almost any seed store. Here we have seen such deadly compounds as dieldrin, chlordane and aldrin, as well as the more potent mixtures of poisons, indiscriminately recommended for use on vegetable crops. It has been known for many years that plants tend to absorb chemical compounds, in addition to their normal nutrient intake, that are in the soil in which they are growing... more recently it has been learned that the roots and tubers of plants retain and store in their tissues an even higher percentage of these compounds. Those who condemn the use of poisons on food crops may appear to be pessimistic, but the chilling truth is that we may have already gone a long way towards contaminating our most fertile farmlands with almost indestructible poisons....Recent surveys have disclosed that probably every meal eaten today in a United States or Canadian restaurant is contaminated to some extent with residues of synthetic pesticides....The question of whether pesticides are contributing to the increase in cancer has fomented a raging debate...There is now a long list of chemical compounds closely related to pesticides and including some of them which

9. *Organic Gardening and Farming,* Vol. 19, No. 11, p. 6.
10. Beatrice Trum Hunter, *Gardening Without Poisons* (London, Hamish Hamilton, Ltd., 1965) p. x.
11. W.G. Smith, *Gardening For Food,* (New York, Scribners, 1972) pp. 4 and 5.

are known to be capable of inducing malignant diseases, according to standard textbooks on chemical carcinogenesis.[12]

The only alternative we have to this growing spiral of poisons is to know what goes into our soil as well as on our plates, and the ideal way to do this *now* is to become part of a community garden. For there you come closest to that delicate human balance we sought in our intentional community between individualism and communalism. One has the privacy of one's own plot to experiment with methods and rhythms entirely one's own, in the greater structure of the group, making possible the intense "contact high" of group effort plus the larger educational and organizational resources of the whole. Private companies, cities and towns, churches, and school systems that sponsor community gardens provide needed classes in organics as well as such facilities as canning centers and root cellars for preserving and storing vegetables that the individual gardener could not possibly duplicate. The group support of individuals working toward the same goal provides a momentum that ensures regularity and constancy of effort right up through post-harvest cleanup. And there is always the tacit example of an expert or demonstration garden nearby to observe in all stages, which creates a silent standard and provides inspiration.

With our present knowledge of the pesticide spiral, we are morally obligated to our planet, if not to ourselves, to grow at least part of our own food, and community gardening is the best way for a beginner to embark on a more self-sufficient lifestyle. Group gardening can transform society from the roots, because our very mode of perceiving the world is changed after a gardening season. By growing our own food organically we see the interconnectedness of all natural systems and thus learn to see ourselves as part of a magnificent ecological interdependence, rather than as isolated individuals. We come to see that we are beautifully and intimately related to one another as well as to the soil, and the recognition of this relatedness can, at its best, come in the grand mystical realization of unity that poets, philosophers, and theologians have heralded for centuries; at its least, the mere intellectual realization of such unity is extremely humbling. One gardening season can end the feeling of human isolation that the Existentialists labeled "alienation," the feeling that pervades our urban areas and manifests itself in increased crime rates and defense budgets.

One gardening season makes it clear to the beginning organic gardener (and tacitly underscores for all of us) that both the root system and the aerial parts of a plant are intimately connected to the insect life in both spheres. If the ratio or harmony of insect life is disturbed, then the plant will begin to wither. By increasing the soil activity through composting and manuring, we increase the health of the

12. Ralph S. Widrig, *Sea Breezes and Vegetable Gardening,* (Nova Scotia, Kentville, 1967) p. 116, 117.

plant and ultimately our own health by eating vitamin-packed plant foods.[13] One gardening season proves that the soil is alive and but a single organ of the complex living whole of the planet; the proper care of our own small plot of soil has a universal effect on the health of the planet and our collective mismanagement of this vital soil organ can turn the earth into a corpse. This realization isn't something easily articulated by the first-season gardener; it is rather an instinctive sensing that pervades and eventually changes one's way of seeing. Experiencing the interrelatedness of phenomena cures the feeling of alienation and makes us newly aware that all life is precious; our realization of the teeming life at the roots of the plant goes to the very roots of our being to change our perception of the entire cosmos, ensuring the continuation of a newly disclosed harmony. Who could ask for more?

13. Heinz Grotzke, "What Biodynamics is All About," *Organic Gardening and Farming*, June 1975, pp. 58-61.

Roots and Growth of the Movement

CHAPTER 1

History of
Community Gardening

Community gardening came to the United States from Europe, where there are records of flourishing systems known as allotment gardens as early as 1731. In Great Britain, rents for a plot on allotment sites, most often privately owned, were as high as one guinea a year, a considerable part of a man's wages, thus giving rise to the colloquial name "guinea garden." These "guinea gardens" were not laid out in monotonous rectilinear plots but showed a great deal of imagination and aesthetic sophistication (Fig. 1) that only the oldest community gardens here in the states boast. Boston's Fenway Gardens are one of these. This suggests that such allotment systems were older than any records show.

An existing record of this period in Birmingham, England shows that appreciation of the beneficial aspects of community gardening is startlingly similar to ours today:

> from the west end of this area (north of the town centre) we enjoy a pleasing and lively summer-view over a considerable tract of land laid out in small gardens. This mode of applying plots of ground, in the immediate vicinity of the town, is highly beneficial to the inhabitants....They promote healthful exercise and rational enjoyment among families of the artisans; and, with good management, produce an ample supply of those wholesome vegetable stores, which are comparatively seldom tasted by the middling classes when they have to be purchased.[1]

The peak of "guinea gardens" occurred between 1820 and 1830, after which the sale of much private land for industrial growth caused the decline of the system. The industrial revolution took its toll on recreational space, and certain prominent industrialists, seeing the need to improve the living conditions of their workers, provided allotment space when setting up their factories. The Cadbury brothers of chocolate fame were among the first to do this.

The Allotments Acts of 1887 and 1890, and the Local Government Act of 1894, were England's acknowledgment of the human necessity to be close to the earth, despite industrialism. Sanitary Authorities in every borough were now required by law to provide allotment space where demand existed. The Small Holdings and

---

1. James Drake, *A Picture of Birmingham* (pub. 1825) excerpted by H. Thorpe, E.B. Galloway, and L.M. Evans, in *From Allotments to Leisure Gardens* (Birmingham, England, 1976) p. 2.

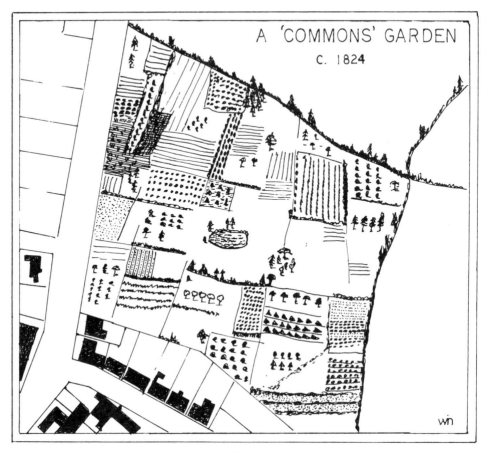

A 'COMMONS' GARDEN
C. 1824

FIGURE 1

Allotments Acts of 1907 and 1908 cemented this obligation, providing citizens without private access to gardening impressive plots of 500 square yards each. World War I brought an increased amount of land in England under cultivation and by 1922, plot size was decreased to 300 square yards, a figure which is generally the standard European allotment in use today.

Allotments flourished in times of war and depression. The years 1918 and 1944 were peaks of the movement, the second being stimulated by England's "Dig for Victory" campaign in the second world war. There were three types of sites for allotments: private, statutory, and temporary. When cities or boroughs purchased private or temporary sites for provision of plots according to the Allotments Acts, they became statutory or permanent sites. Having permanent sites that grow richer year after year has made a great contribution to the success and continuing growth of community gardens in England and is the one factor that could seal the future success of the movement in the United States. Even the English sites classified as

This drawing shows the English penchant for improvisation; the hut, outfitted with curtains and a crate for an annex, serves as a tool shed, with a compost heap to one side. A plotter has moved this "Anderson shelter," a quonset-like building that looks as if it were made from an enormous barrel, to the edge of his/her plot, and the result is a neat, homey little nook for the tools.[2]

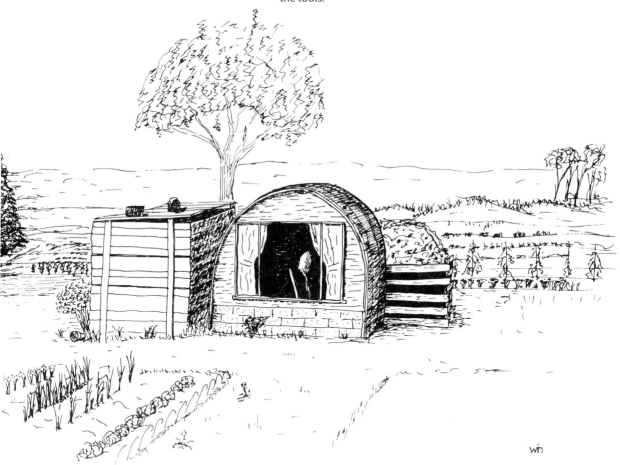

2. H. Thorpe, "The Homely Allotment: From Rural Dole to Urban Amenity: A Neglected Aspect of Urban Land Use," *Geography,* Vol. 60, Part 3, (July 1975), p. 179.

Temporary have leases as long as forty years, and the majority of private sites are owned by plotholders individually or by societies or limited companies formed by the plotholders; thus plots can pass by deed from generation to generation.

In 1965, one-fifth of all allotment land in Great Britain lay unused; by 1976, present demand was one-fifth greater than the number of tenants on allotments,[3] or "leisure gardens" as they are now officially called.

Growth of the leisure-garden movement in Europe is aided not only by several thousand horticultural and allotment societies in Britain alone, but also by an International Leisure Gardeners Association, which holds congresses. In September 1976, for the first time in history, the United States was represented at one of these congresses. One delegate represented Gardens For All, Inc. in Shelburne, Vermont, and the other was from the Bureau of Outdoor Recreation. Other delegates came from Britain, Wales, France, Belgium, Germany, and other parts of Western Europe. Because of this organized encouragement, there are now more than one million leisure gardens in Great Britain, about one-half million in West Germany, 36,000 in Switzerland and about 30,000 in Sweden. There are thousands more in Denmark, France and the Netherlands.[4] The movement in the United States would be similarly spurred by a national organization that could unite the 1200 individual programs across the country by means of yearly congresses, newsletters, and informational material.

These individual community gardens across the country have their origins in the Victory Gardens of World Wars I and II, and were direct descendants of Europe's allotments system. A few prototypes started to ease the strain of the Depression. The Fenway Gardens in Boston, the Oxford Paper Company Gardens in Rumford, Maine, and the Staley Gardens in Decatur, Illinois, are among the earliest continuous community gardens in the United States; and the Cleveland Public School system started its program in 1904.

Victory Garden programs were organized in 1942 through the public schools by PTA committees. The gardening experience embodies all the patriotic virtues: democracy, equality, and individualism. Thus the Victory Gardens were the peak of the community garden movement until the 1970's. Yields from the gardens were consumed directly or sold and the proceeds used for the benefit of men in the armed services. Contests and awards by companies like Burpee, Sears Roebuck and Calvert Distillers stimulated the gardening effort until, in many areas of the country, there were far fewer plot spaces than there were applicants—who had to be chosen by lottery. Newspapers ran columns on war gardening, country clubs gave over their fairways and cemeteries their expansion space to Victory Gardens.[5] Patriotic spirit

3. H. Thorpe, E.B. Galloway, and L.M. Evans, op. cit., p. 28.
4. Gardens For All, Spring Press Release, 1977, p. 2.
5. *Decatur Herald,* March 30, 1965.

rooted allotment gardening firmly in the American tradition where it flourished into the late forties, then gradually declined in the fifties and sixties. Private corporation and school garden programs continued.

Now, the Victory Garden spirit has been rekindled, and the spark has been struck mainly through the efforts of Gardens For All, a non-profit foundation established in 1972 to promote community gardening in the United States. Located in Shelburne, Vermont, it was given impetus by forty families in the Burlington area who needed help starting a community garden. By 1973, Gardens For All had enlarged the scope to include 540 plots; by 1974, 750; and by 1975, there were 1150 plots on twenty-seven different sites in a radius of seven miles from the heart of Burlington.

Gardens For All has become the national clearinghouse for the community garden movement by maintaining files on 1300 garden programs, to whom they send progress questionnaires periodically. They direct organizers to already existing programs, promote community gardens through public relations campaigns, assist the media, and put out highly professional manuals to assist organizers in starting gardens in the community and school systems. The manuals are the definitive source of data on organizing community gardens; nearly all the principles of organization in the succeeding pages are based on Gardens For All's manual.

In 1975, Gardens For All reported that every one of the fifty states had community garden programs. Pennsylvania's "Anti-inflationary Seed and Gardening Program" put it far in the lead with assistance to over 300,000 gardeners in 1976, with 5600 community gardens on state land. Twenty-two percent of the respondents to GFA's survey were organized in 1976, and forty-eight percent of these projects will expand their plot totals in 1977, and this is without the officially sanctioned victory push as in World War II. Gardens For All has been a tremendously unifying force behind the burgeoning growth of the 1970's.

In their 1976 survey of group garden coordinators and manual buyers throughout the country, Gardens For All reported many significant trends, some of which are summarized by Figure 2. Most of the gardens have between 26 to 100 plots, the average plot being in the 100- to 750-square foot range. Though most gardens from survey results were made up of 25 to 100 persons, twenty-one of the programs had more than 500 gardeners and nine reported more than 1200. Gardening classes are available in sixty percent of the programs, while canning and preserving classes are held by thirty-five percent.[6] In these cases, community gardening is a vehicle to reach people of varied persuasions and lifestyles with education into more organic and ecological living.

In addition to education, some gardens sell produce, praying-mantis eggs, and

6. GFA 1976 Survey results.

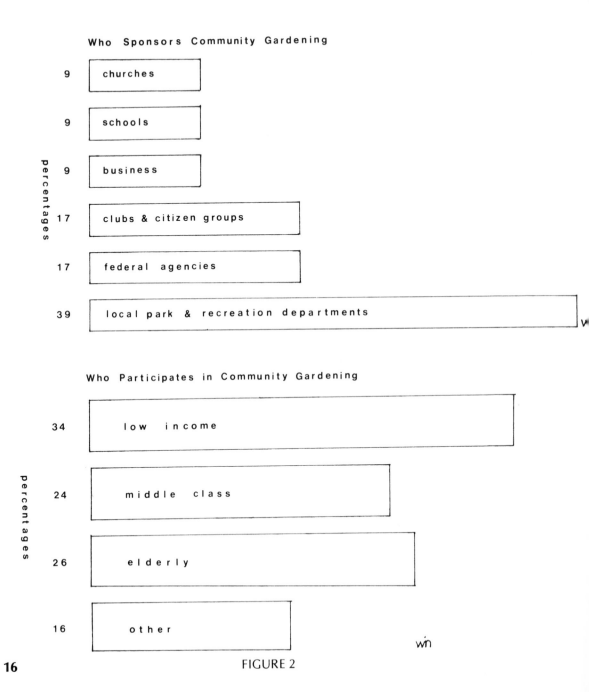

Who Sponsors Community Gardening

percentages	
9	churches
9	schools
9	business
17	clubs & citizen groups
17	federal agencies
39	local park & recreation departments

Who Participates in Community Gardening

percentages	
34	low income
24	middle class
26	elderly
16	other

16   FIGURE 2

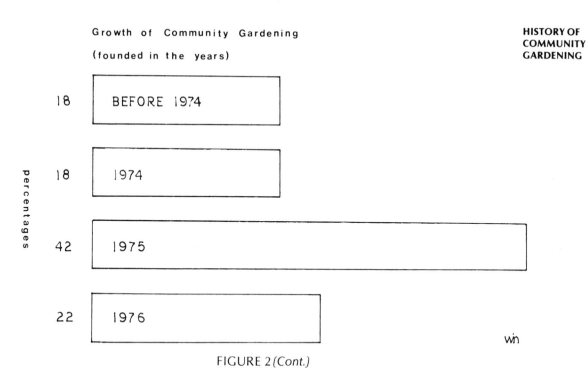

Growth of Community Gardening

(founded in the years)

FIGURE 2 *(Cont.)*

foster recycling programs. Harvest festivals, newsletters, garden shows, and old-fashioned farm stands are additional spirit lifters and serve to wind up the season with good feelings in September.[7]

Looking to Europe's examples of statutory allotment sites and even temporary or private sites with long leases, Gardens For All is encouraging the development of permanent sites in the United States. Such permanence would not only stimulate participation in the movement but would also assure the growing fertility of the land over years of proper management and thus the increased quality of produce. It would make the national communications network, GFA's major task, more efficient because keeping tabs on programs that change coordinators and location every few years is almost impossible. The permanent site plan in Great Britain allows for the most sophisticated aesthetic layouts and recreation facilities, including clubhouses or central gathering and entertaining facilities (Fig. 3). United States group gardening would warrant permanent site plan legislation because it is low-cost or self-sustaining recreation, the plot fees paying yearly expenses. In addition, group

7. GFA *News About Community Gardening*—1976.

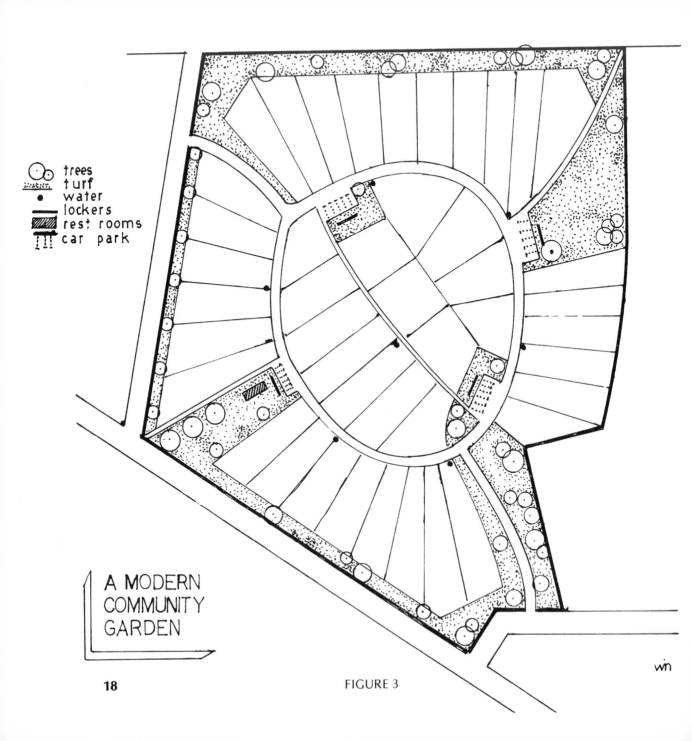

○○ trees
turf
• water
lockers
rest rooms
car park

A MODERN
COMMUNITY
GARDEN

wn

18   FIGURE 3

gardens have revitalized neighborhoods, strengthened families, and helped to cut crime rates.

Because of community gardening's proven record in these respects, Congress allocated $1.5 million in the spring of 1976 to the Department of Agriculture to encourage gardens in the cities.[8] Community gardening has achieved a sort of official respectability. Thus it seems that the climate is now right for a final push from environmental groups like GFA and concerned individual gardeners, through letters to representatives, to bring a permanent site plan into being. And then we can watch those gardens really take off, as gardeners unleash their imaginations year after year on the same site that grows richer and richer.

Another goal for Gardens For All is a national newsletter to aid communication and lay the foundation for a national organization like Europe's International Leisure Gardeners Association. They have been filling the gaps by their surveys, reports, questionnaires, and letters, but the burgeoning expansion of programs would be strongly supported by the unity that can come from a chartered association or a regular channel of communication. Whatever direction the movement takes, however, Gardens For All will remain its heart; this is the source of needed and continued encouragement for all of us learning to simplify and purify our lives through new contact with the soil.

8. *New York Times,* October 17, 1976, p. 41.

CHAPTER 2

Horticulture Therapy

Perhaps the most dramatic examples of the purifying and transforming effect of gardening are found in working models of a new branch of rehabilitation called hortitherapy. These models, often in the form of community gardens, are found in mental hospitals, prisons, universities, ghettos, inner-city schools, homes for the aged, and convalescent homes, everywhere pointing up the vast restorative value responsibility for natural life cycles can have. Charles A. Lewis is a Horticulturist with the Morton Arboretum in Lisle, Illinois. He writes that "some scientists believe man has a primal need for plants, hearkening back to the early days of this planet when green plants were the sole form of life. Through photosynthesis, plants consumed carbon dioxide and expelled oxygen, modifying the atmosphere until it became hospitable for oxygen-breathing forms of life to begin their evolutionary journey. Man emerged in a green world, and its memory may be programmed in his genes."[1]

Knowledge of the restorative value of caring for plants is not new with Kaplan, Lewis, and other psychologists and horticulturists who have recently publicized the link between nature and mental health. In 1768 Benjamin Rush made the sweeping claim that gardening could cure the mentally ill; in 1806, mental patients in Spanish hospitals gardened therapeutically; and at about the same time in northern Scotland a Dr. Gregory maintained he could cure insanity by requiring patients to do farm work.[2]

Today's hortitherapists make no such claims, but there is growing realization that the artificial environment of cities combined with the structuring of waking activity by the clock rather than the innate rhythms of sun, moon, and seasons, contribute to fatigue, inefficiency, and alienation.[3] And all it takes to alleviate the alienation that results in vandalizing and disfiguring inner-city neighborhoods is a few flowers, strategically placed. On the worst block in New York's Upper West

1. Charles A. Lewis, "People-Plant Interaction: A New Horticultural Perspective," *American Horticulturist,* 52(2): (Summer 1973), pp. 18-25.

2. J. Gaylin, "Green-Thumb Therapy For The Handicapped," *Psychology Today,* Vol. 9 (April, 1976), p. 118.

3. Edward Stainbrook, "Man's Psychic Needs For Nature," *National Parks and Conservation Magazine,* Vol. 47, No. 9 (1973), p. 22.

Side, one flowerbox of geraniums and English ivy transformed the neighborhood into "the street of the flowerboxes" in just one summer's time. The lone flowerbox, installed by a starry-eyed couple new to the neighborhood who were about to have their first child and settle in for good, inspired the competition of others all up and down the street. Then the resultant added color of the new flowerboxes spurred tenants to put in fresh curtains and polish their brass doorknobs. "Airmail" (garbage dumped from upper-story windows) stopped, and outdoor garbage and trash cans were provided by newly interested landlords. The perpetual gang wars between Black and Puerto-Rican youths ceased as the boys began to turn their energies to painting flowerboxes and providing for plants. West 94th Street was transformed and restored pride to the entire neighborhood.[4]

An annual flower contest, sponsored since 1961 by the New York City Housing Authority among its 600,000 public housing tenants, has resulted in a surprising reduction in vandalism of trees and shrubs planted by the city.[5] Charles A. Lewis has been a judge of this contest and writes of his experience:

Unless one looked closely, he would see only the obvious: gardens in low-income areas, beautification, a cosmetic cover over social wounds. These were my own impressions as I started my first judging experience nine years ago. But in talking with contestants, I began to hear echoes of a much deeper kind of involvement. Remember, the housing projects are in some of the toughest areas of New York, where crime and vandalism are high and life presents a harsh struggle from cradle to grave. One contestant told me, "This is the first creative thing I have done in my life", and added that she had gone to the library to study every book available on gardening. In lower Manhattan, a Spanish-speaking woman proudly said, "They told me that you couldn't grow flowers on Avenue D, but I wanted to try. Now you should see how the old folks come out every day to enjoy the flowers." I particularly remember an older woman who, with a group of children, had produced a garden with flowers, vegetables, and even a cotton plant. She had carefully labeled each type of plant because, she explained, it was important for children to know the names of all the plants. In letters to the Authority, tenants said, "...what is more important is everyone getting to know each other, everyone smiles and discusses our garden, they worry over too much rain, not enough rain, they're all so pleased that children are interested in caring, not destroying. From early morning till late at night you can see neighbors leaning over the garden fence. It has become the center spot of our court where everyone is a friend."...After a few years, the Housing Authority became aware of unexpected benefits emanating from the garden contest. Vandalism was reduced in areas where there were gardens; indeed, there evolved behavior which is the very antithesis of vandalism. Tenants began approaching the Housing Authority for

4. Adapted from Peggy Mann, "Miracle of the Flower Boxes," *The Reader's Digest*, 103, (July '73), pp. 106-110.

5. C. Leon, "The Healing Power of Gardening," *House and Garden*, 148, (Feb. '76), p. 134.

permission to help landscape the buildings. In several projects they contributed their own funds to create spring gardens for bloom before the summer contest plantings. Some asked permission to install planters which they would maintain in the lobbies of their buildings. As a result of the contest, garden clubs have been formed and the Housing Authority is looking for ways to develop indoor gardening activities through the winter. Thus it seems that the experience of gardening can help residents achieve a proprietary sense over their buildings and grounds.[6]

Lewis speculates on the reasons for this improvement:

....A ghetto dweller, cut off from adequate means of self-expression and self-identification, finds that he can grow plants in front of his stone house for all to see, the flower symbolizing his uniqueness and individuality. Further, what starts as a representation of self, becomes a generous gift as others, often unknown, share in its pleasure. Plants are non-threatening in a hostile world; they respond equally to all, without reference to age, race, social class. In an ambience of failure, they offer paths to conspicuous success.[7]

The improvements that flowers make on a neighborhood's appearance combined with the new status responsibility for life, no matter how small, confers, increase the self-esteem of the tenants, thus reducing their destructive tendencies. Along with new self-esteem comes the security given by the assurance of permanence and duration; the flowerboxes of West 94th Street provided a glimpse of nature's timeless cycles amidst the constant clamorous change of gang warfare and uprooted tenants and flying garbage. Edward Stainbrook, chairman of the Department of Human Behavior at the University of Southern California School of Medicine, clearly expresses this need:

Another subtle human need for the natural environment has to do with the experience of permanency and change. To support his unconscious striving for immortality (because of his fear of death), man needs the sense of security provided by the timeless duration of nature. As changes in contemporary society accelerate and multiply, the need for natural surroundings becomes increasingly important. Moments of crisis are reduced to manageable dimensions when seen from the perspective of enduring nature.[8]

Besides being comforted by a glimpse of nature's timelessness, the hortitherapy patient can generalize new plant skills to his or her immediate future. The National Council for Therapy and Rehabilitation through Horticulture, established in 1973 and composed of more than 350 hospitals, universities, and other organizations, reports that over seventy-five percent of the graduates of U.S. institutions for hortitherapy have gone into jobs related to their training or have found their horticulture

6. Lewis, op. cit.

7. Ibid.

8. E. Stainbrook, op. cit., p. 23.

skills have made employment more accessible to them. Among the National Council's hundreds of examples are the following success stories: One seventy-year-old graduate built a greenhouse in her backyard to sell bedding plants and dish gardens to supplement social security; two mildly retarded brothers work in commercial greenhouses in their hometown; one visually handicapped individual with poor coordination opened a greenhouse to earn a living; others are in buildings and grounds maintenance, nurseries, and parks.[9]

A former warden of Statesville Penitentiary in Illinois has reported to the National Council that he has been able to rehabilitate some of the toughest psychological criminals only by means of hortitherapy. Working with plants lowers aggressiveness, making gardening a potential medium for social interaction. Martin Cotton works with delinquent teenage boys in Pennsylvania's state institution for juveniles, in a hortitherapy program established in November 1974. Their crimes range from "incorrigibility to murder," and since Cotton has worked with them, he has observed a remarkable loss of aggression:

> The greenhouse measures sixteen feet by twelve feet. It is equipped with three large tables, a utility cabinet and a desk and chair. At peak times we have ten to fifteen students working together in close quarters. In the entire time the program has been operational we have not had a single incident of aggression of a verbal or physical nature. We have worked with rival gang members, students who were enemies, blacks and whites. All these were situations where fights or, at the very least, verbal confrontations could occur. None did.[10]

This lowering of aggression in delinquents becomes sociability in non-institutionalized gardeners, making community gardening score high on measures of social meaning. Rachel Kaplan devised such measures for determining the psychological benefits of community gardening and private gardening,[11] finding that a major reason people garden in a community context is because of the opportunity for social interaction. Flower growers scored higher in terms of sustained interest benefits than did the gardeners who grew no flowers,[12] which Kaplan attributes to the factor of fascination, cited in our introduction. Fascination counts for more staying power than the more material motives of saving money or eating well, manifested in vegetable gardens. The sustained interest engendered by fascination

9. *People and Plants,* Pamphlet of the National Council for Therapy and Rehabilitation Through Horticulture.

10. M. Cotton, "Horticultural Therapy," *Horticulture,* Vol. 53, (Sept. 1975), p. 24.

11. R. Kaplan, "Some Psychological Benefits of Gardening," *Environment and Behavior,* Vol. 5, No. 2 (June 1973).

12. Ibid., p. 156.

is the reason a few flowerboxes burgeoned into a miracle on West 94th Street in a single summer.

Kaplan also had a tangible benefits scale, which vegetable gardeners scored high in. She found that beginners grow vegetables and tangible benefits are very important in luring them into the science of plants. Older, more experienced gardeners plant flowers, scoring higher on sustained interest measurements.[13] This finding is in keeping with the successive involvement in any art form; first there is the self-consciousness, the plan of how one might impose oneself on the content of the specific medium. Then, as one is pulled further into the project by the power of the medium, there is a self-forgetting, culminating in William James' "involuntary attention," or Kaplan's "fascination." In our first attempt at community gardening, outlined in the introduction, we were concerned with aesthetics more than tangible benefits, but not because we had reached the state of fascination. We were too self-concerned, and wanted to impose our mark on the landscape, thereby creating the fiasco of our fenceless tea garden.

Our next garden was built with the tangible benefit of high yields of various kinds of beans to dry and take us through the winter as the highest priority, and the necessary attention to nature to produce that yield caused the self-forgetting, the hiatus in the inner stream of chatter that assailed most of us when we weren't gardening, that was the prelude to our fascination. Now, although I grow vegetables for tangible benefits, the major part of my garden is given over to flowers. I have come full circle back to aesthetics, but as a changed person with a whole different way of seeing the world as a result of the successive steps of involvement given by the first two communal gardens. Now I can give myself over in fascination to nature, rather than struggling to mold nature to my plan. Hortitherapy is just this progression of psychic steps that achieve self-forgetting, producing the immediate rewards of expanded states of consciousness through fascination as well as the more long-range effect of humility. One who has forgotten oneself long enough to become fascinated in a new medium is a more humble person, easier to live with. The gang members of West 94th Street who exchanged their chains and knives for trowels and petunias were humble enough to say to the new mother who had started the flowerbox transformation: "A flower is sort of like a smile."[14]

13. Ibid., p. 159.
14. Peggy Mann, op. cit., p. 110.

CHAPTER 3

Gardening
in the Schools

Gardening is proving its restorative value in the school system as well as in rehabilitative institutions. Children and young adults are much more open to its values than are adults, the children of primary grades being most receptive to gardening's lure and benefits. This is probably because the element of fascination is more prevalent and contagious in younger children. Teachers and parents involved in the school gardening programs are taught to encourage this fascination and curiosity by answering the numerous whys of plant science with "I don't know, let's find out,"[1] to take the child further into the world of horticulture. The further the child goes, the more all-encompassing the world of plants becomes, until just about every subject in the school curriculum can be entered by the garden path. Peter J. Wotowiec, Supervisor of the Horticulture Department in the Cleveland Public School system, which sponsors a sophisticated 73-year-old school garden program, confirms this:

> My philosophy is that horticulture education is not a subject in itself, but a real-life laboratory for the application of just about all the academic skills and knowledge acquired in the academic classrooms. This fits our school system philosophy and since we reinforce what is done in the classrooms in Math, Science, Social Studies, etc., we have the acceptance of the classroom teachers as well.

Correlation with these other subjects can be emphasized in the following ways:[2]

1. Social Studies
   a. Studying how people store food for use
   b. Studying world regions — i.e. desert, jungle, plains, etc.
   c. Listing Community helpers: Extension Service Agent, U.S. Department of Agriculture, garbage collector, trash collector (for compost or leaves), etc.
   d. Studying how the needs of the community are met: soil conservation, food preparation, marketing, water conservation
   e. Map study

1. Chevron Chemical Company, *A Child's Garden,* A Guide For Parents and Teachers, (San Francisco, Chevron Chemical Company, Ortho Division, 1974) Adapted from p. 9.

2. Ibid. p. 8.

2. Mathematics
   a. Measuring plant growth
   b. Measuring amounts of materials needed to construct mini-gardens (mini-gardens are individual small plots for each child)
   c. Estimating and checking planting dates in various geographical regions
   d. Making graphs and charts
3. Language arts
   a. Writing original stories of the project activities
   b. Recording daily progress of the studies and experiences
   c. Using references, supplementary books, journals, newspapers, etc.
   d. Presenting group reports and discussions
4. Art
   a. Making a mural of the acitivity
   b. Painting posters and slogans for community involvement
   c. Planning displays for the P.T.A.
   d. Making paper sculpture and clay containers

At the high school level, an introductory economics class could study the history of gardening in the United States and Europe, noting how the popularity of gardening has corresponded to periods of economic hardship, recession, or depression. They could also study the various shortages that these periods of popularity produce, such as the seed and canning jar lid shortages of the seventies. What will a nationwide drive toward gardening do to vegetable prices in the summer; what will it do to local suppliers, or to the overall yearly production estimates of companies like DelMonte? Could permanent site legislation, if passed in the United States, create more jobs for those with horticulture skills? Could food production be localized through the promotion of community gardening, thus eliminating shipping costs?

There are many more areas that gardening can tie into, several of them more suitable to the college level. Hortitherapy is operable at the grade and high school levels, though more suitable as a discipline at the university level. Let's look at how it operates. Peter Wotowiec has this to say about the restorative effects of the gardening program:

> We have seen numerous instances where participation in a teacher directed gardening program resulted in significant changes in a child's behavior. Vandalism, absenteeism, and tensions have been reduced in many instances.
>
> School gardening is not a panacea for social problems of children, but if properly managed it provides a viable medium to reach and help children with such problems.

The school program definitely has effects on the outer community; the children would probably be thrilled to know that their interest makes waves. Imagine how

27

proud a child would be to bring new-found skills home and have parents respond by starting their own first garden. From Wotowiec's observations, this might very well happen:

> As to effects on the outer community, I can cite two examples: the homes in the vicinity of our school gardens tend to be much better maintained than those a few streets away. Also, the Seed Trade Association has noted that mail order sales of seeds in the metropolitan Cleveland area is significantly higher than in other cities of comparable size. Furthermore, the high interest in our adult horticulture courses indicates that there is a carryover from school gardening.

The Cleveland Public School system has an enviable community garden program, with more than 4,000 children renting plots on ninety-two acres of land in the City of Cleveland. The primary grades use home plots, supervised by a visiting teacher throughout the summer. Some of the kindergarten plots are four by six feet, yielding a 10¢ mixture of flowers and radishes or some other never-fail vegetable. Second-graders spend 25¢ each for a summer kit composed of a tomato, zinneas, beans, and gladiolas. Third-graders have a larger choice, ranging from 25¢ to $2 kits, as well as the option of gardening on a community site.

Community gardens are located on tract land broken into parcels of one and a half to eight acres each, open to students who live within walking distance of their specified site. The sites provide plots of approximately six by ten feet for third graders and up to ten by thirty for senior high students. Conveniently, most of these sites are located nearby a school, so that there is a regularly scheduled program of horticultural classes from early spring through fall for gardeners. They pay a small fee for the plot, tools, seeds, plants and fertilizer. In the summer, when garden classes cannot be scheduled after school as they are in the spring and fall, the students meet twice a week for classes by the tract teacher in charge assisted by one or more parttime teachers. During the last of August, the gardeners get to display their vegetables and flowers in a city-wide Garden Fair. Even posters and essays can qualify for some sort of prize, and every working gardener is rewarded with tickets to one Cleveland Indians baseball game and to the Cayuhoga County Fair. So everyone wins, the students perhaps doing more growing than the vegetables and flowers during a season.

Recognition is important for student gardeners of all ages, and teachers find that if they group peers together and maintain controlled competition, the season's garden will be a social success. In addition to the recognition of peers, a gardener who brings home produce to contribute to family meals gets parent approval and has the assurance that his work is appreciated.

The high school students have a number of projects to choose from, all

supplying vocational skills in landscaping, environmental management, florist management, nursery and schoolyard maintenance. These skills could lead easily into such college majors as Landscape Architecture, City Planning, and Botany. Courses of study which are under the aegis of the Horticulture Department and which provide on-the-job work experience in their final year are: Environmental Management, Agricultural Products, Small Animal Care, Horticulture Mechanics, and Ornamental Horticulture. Ornamental Horticulture is a three-year program, all the others are two years—usually junior and senior years.

Until then, pupils from fourth grade on can join a voluntary Environmental Education Program that devises ways to clean up and preserve the environment. Looking at its list of objectives, one can see how the organization is designed to relate to all of the other academic areas of the curriculum:

Objectives
1. To motivate students toward an awareness of current environmental problems.
2. To establish programs involving student active participation in schoolgrounds clean-up projects, lawn, flower, shrub and tree planting and maintenance activities.
3. To develop a basic understanding of ecology with specific emphasis on the importance of plants in our environment.
4. To develop good citizenship and socially desirable behavior in school-age students.
5. To demonstrate, by example, the importance of beauty and how it affects our every way of life.
6. To develop better work habits through active work assignment projects on the schoolgrounds or in the neighborhood.

Besides ongoing rewards such as prize plants, and achievement certificates, the students are spurred on in the organization because of simple peer pressure. It is an established form of participation—the thing to do—for many of the achievement-oriented, and has perhaps reached the status of a good habit with members of long-standing who joined in the fourth or fifth grade. There is adequate recognition from the tangible results of improved school grounds, as well as from *The Cleveland Press*'s ongoing publication of awards and activities. The *Press* has an annual commitment to provide the program with printed materials and to sponsor related events.

Much of the teaching of gardening and plant science can be done inside so that the horticulture program continues throughout the winter. The upper elementary classes have lessons and projects in potting softwood cuttings, planting Dutch bulbs, sprouting an onion core, planting and forcing paper white narcissus, making a winter terrarium out of a peanut-butter jar, learning to recognize different types of Christmas trees and greens, forcing Easter lilies, and learning to distinguish rocks and soils. Most of these lessons are coordinated with an FM broadcast on the school radio station, called the Green Thumb Club. During the broadcast, students participate in the classroom; the station sends all supplies for the lesson prior to broadcast time. Thus the teacher who may not be a plant science expert gets expert assistance at the time of each lesson.

Clearly the students of the Cleveland system are fortunate to have the most sophisticated public school horticulture program in the country. It is not only well planned and organized with frequent rewards and reinforcement built right into its organization, but, with its 73-year history, it has also been well tested. And it is administered and coordinated by experts with a rare blend of horticultural and human expertise, who care about the students' self-esteem.

Because it started in 1904, Cleveland has the jump on other school systems, but some have the added strength of state support. Alabama has a statewide agribusiness program with 456 projects located throughout the state. Many of these projects serve the public schools, with plots located as near the school grounds as possible, free plants and seed, and horticultural advice. Student motivation and participation is high, and the programs have no vandalism. There seems to be more pride of possession among younger gardeners than is found on adult sites, so that a contingent of the children keep a watchful eye on the entire site, thus discouraging vandalism before it starts.

In experiments with children in a community garden situation, it has been shown that peer influence counts for a lot. As Kaplan found with the older, more experienced gardeners, younger gardeners care more about aesthetics than tangible benefits from produce. Perhaps this is because they are provided for by their parents, so growing their own food has little meaning for them. But it is more likely that the element of fascination is even more powerful in young children, for they are the ones who love to plant flowers while the high school students plant vegetables. In the Children's Adventure Garden at the University of California at Berkeley, three-dimensional structures were built such as raised island flower beds, a bean-house frame, and tripods for climbing plants, and the children's fascination with the plants' adherence to these structural forms contributed greatly to the project's success. The bean house had rows of snap beans climbing its trellised sides and roof. The children could go in and out, and it became a center of activity, eventually the location for the bulletin board with its weekly check lists of what each individual gardener needed to do next.[3]

Along with immense fascination, the children exhibited growing cooperative behavior as the project progressed. The same interesting blend of individualism and cooperative effort was apparent in the conglomeration of little plots as on adult sites, yet there was growth from territorial and possessive behavior to sharing.

3. Adapted from Chevron Chemical Company, op. cit., p. 2.

31

Towards the end of the season, children shared the plots with their siblings or friends and even carefully tended the plots of friends who left for a few days' vacation.[4]

Children are especially receptive to community gardening or horticulture of any kind. Schools that integrate horticulture with an academic curriculum are tapping a vast resource for environmental protection, because a responsibility for living things can become a good habit if instilled young. And the excitement at the first spring seedling's uncurling through the surface of the soil intensifies with every year of growth with plants, so that a person who has worked a plot since kindergarten gets an extra boost each spring. Would that we all could have gone to such schools to grow green symbols of our own yearly awakenings.

4. Ibid., p. 2.

Garden Profiles

LISTEN

Marcia Boutin was only six when she began working with her mother and brothers and sisters in their first Victory Garden in 1943. The family dooryard was her first community garden site, where neighbors would come and share the work and harvest with the large Boutin family, and the kids were so excited that they all wore Army hats whenever they worked in the garden. They were too young to understand the economic connection between their garden and the war, but they made a literal connection nonetheless, probably because the contagious spirit of patriotism was so akin to and harmonious with the gardening spirit. The three years of Victory gardening, 1943, 1944, and 1945, made such a profound impression on Marcia that thirty years later she connected her vivid memories with the glaring need she saw among Lebanon, New Hampshire's poor, and started LISTEN.

LISTEN (Lebanon In Service To Each Neighbor) is a non-profit corporation formed in 1972 to help low and moderate income citizens pool their resources to better control political, social, and economic decisions which affect them. It is maintained by membership dues of $5 per year and affords its members an impressive array of services: a food co-op, called a food-buying club because of the elitist connotations "co-op" has for some low-income groups, a thrift store, an emergency food program to assist families facing a food crisis, a youth center, a monthly newsletter, a community gardening program, and a resource center. The resource center is composed of two reading rooms stocked with literature on consumer issues, federal programs, gardening, and community organizing. A woodworking and furniture repair shop and an auto mechanics' garage are in the making. Classes in conjunction with the public schools and adult education will utilize the woodworking and auto shops for a work-study program.

Although LISTEN is supported by a combination of sources, Marcia Boutin does an impressive amount of fundraising on her own, enough so that she can envision becoming self-sufficient some day. Three thousand dollars of its annual $18,000 budget is provided by United Way, $2500 by the County, and the rest Marcia raises by membership dues, contributions, and door-knocking campaigns. LISTEN is housed in its own building, a property owned by the LISTEN members themselves who, marshalled by Marcia, went from door to door and held a turkey dinner to raise the down payment. Marcia made the offer, then with complete self-assurance went about organizing the fundraising drive and, two weeks later, came up with the $7500 for the down payment plus $4500 for taxes, water, and renovation. Because the members had to raise the price of the building themselves, they have a greater stake in it which is reflected in the way they all show up to install the latest improvements.

The members have just installed a polyethylene greenhouse along the south wall to grow plants for the gardening program as well as houseplants to sell for LISTEN support. Marcia's biggest and most successful emphasis has been on letting the LISTEN members do their own work, which gives them responsibility and pride in their own programs. If an applicant cannot come up with the annual membership dues, minimal as they are, Marcia lets them join in return for an hour or two of work. This seems to give the member the essential sense of accomplishment and stake in the project to assure its future. There is a level of participation from the LISTEN membership that isn't present in federally funded programs. The remaining $20,000 to pay off the mortgage on their building is the next hurdle the members have to cross, but given the success of the initial two-week drive, members know that Marcia sets serious and practical fundraising goals that aren't beyond them.

The gardening program is LISTEN's only federally-sponsored project, the first community garden in the nation to secure matching funds from the Bureau of Outdoor Recreation to buy a permanent site for community plots and outdoor recreation facilities. These funds were applied for after LISTEN members won their open-space campaign, waged at a public hearing at City Hall to discuss the allocation of $135,000 in Housing and Community Development funds. Two hundred LISTEN members turned up at the hearing and asked that half of the $18,500 total project cost be granted for the purchase of permanent open space for community garden sites as well as for skiing, snowmobiling, and other types of recreation. City councilors were surprised and impressed with the enthusiasm and organization of the campaign and granted the request. Now the Bureau of Outdoor Recreation has matched city monies and LISTEN will buy and improve a five-acre parcel that is ideal for gardening.

The Bureau of Outdoor Recreation's matching funds can only be applied for by a city that has already allocated funds for outdoor recreation. Although the original $9250 from Lebanon's 1976 Community Development funds would cover the cost of acquisition, the $8650 from the BOR plus $600 from the state of New Hampshire is essential for the kind of improvements that will ensure that the site remain a garden. If the purchase were solely the city's investment, the Housing and Development committee could reclaim it at anytime for housing. Since community gardening has been recognized by the BOR as a form of family recreation, more cities can take advantage of the availability of matching funds for permanent sites. LISTEN is turning their site into a model layout that will hopefully stimulate other cities to follow suit. Figure 4 shows its proposed design, which will be completed by the

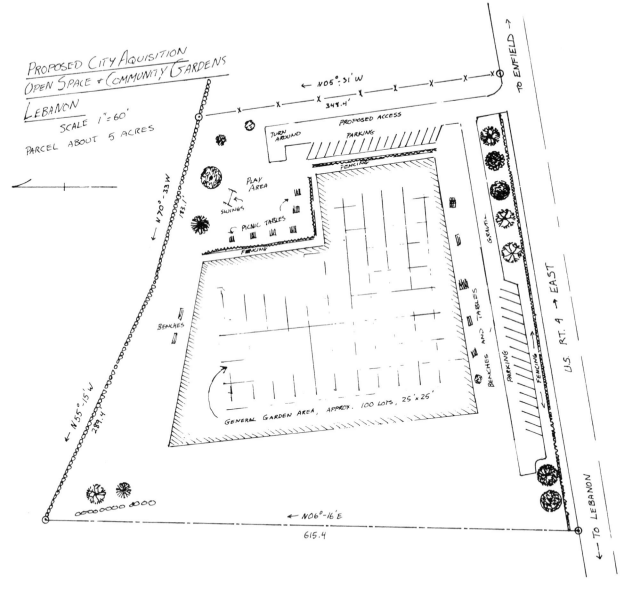

PROPOSED CITY AQUISITION
OPEN SPACE & COMMUNITY GARDENS
LEBANON
SCALE 1"=60'
PARCEL ABOUT 5 ACRES

← NO5°-31'W
348.4'

← TO ENFIELD →

N70°-33'W
153.1'

TURN AROUND
PROPOSED ACCESS
PARKING
FENCING

PLAY AREA
SWINGS
PICNIC TABLES
FENCING

BENCHES

GRAVEL

BENCHES AND TABLES

PARKING

FENCING

U.S. RT. 4 → EAST

N55°-15'W
289.4

GENERAL GARDEN AREA, APPROX. 100 LOTS, 25'×25'

← NO6°-16'E
615.4

← TO LEBANON

FIGURE 4   37

1978 gardening season. It is situated on a major highway so that it should generate at least as much publicity as LISTEN's entire organization has in the past.

Even with this initial large Federal outlay for the permanent site, Marcia continues to try to reduce the program's dependence on the government. For the last few years the gardening project has been supported by Operation Green Thumb, a Federal funding project for gardens. Last year for LISTEN's 107 plots, Marcia budgeted $1200 for site preparation, hoses, and seed, which composed the total cost of a gardening season. The program actually cost only $900 because of the surplus produce sold. This year with the greenhouse, Marcia thinks she can cut the total cost down even lower; with a farm stand or similar fundraising, Marcia envisions self-sufficiency for the garden program in five years' time.

This five-year goal is thoroughly realistic since LISTEN has operated under its decreasing budget each year of the garden program. The success of LISTEN is partially due to this realism in economic goal-setting. Such a five-year plan keeps Marcia and the garden committee from becoming frustrated and impatient during that time. One coordinator I met had had one failure after another in setting up community gardens, canneries, and food programs. He described himself as an impatient man, unable to make realistic goals. He added that if he planned a project, he wanted it done yesterday. Marcia says that she wants it done next year, or five years from now. This realism is impressive in an area as new as community gardening. And this realism isn't just limited to time goals; Marcia seems to know the secret of successful grassroots accomplishment. The way to get people involved is to let them see a program through in all its aspects. There is no split between administration and menial labor; the workers are the administration and make policy. And economics is the backbone of grassroots activity. Raising the funds—from door-knocking to drafting funding proposals to the BOR—is the members' responsibility.

And the rewards of such responsibility are often intangible; moments together on the site can be more sustaining than the harvest. Invariably, the garden situation produced miracles of communication among old enemies that no other context could. Thirty low-income families from the same housing project who argued and fought together for years in the contexts of housing and welfare which Marcia observed them in, would work together harmoniously on LISTEN's garden site for the entire season. Another miracle gardeners reported enthusiastically was the breaking down of social hierarchies on the site. One gardener said that on the street, he wouldn't dream of talking to someone who had a better job than he did, but in a garden he mixes happily with professionals and makes new friends. Plants respond regardless of economic categories, and for some low-income people, the soil is the first medium they have worked in that displays this kind of equality. Their hidden talents become visible on the garden site and they find they actually have some knowledge that they can give to a doctor or lawyer working beside them. There is a constant exchange of ideas, recipes, garden tips, canning short-cuts, political and moral views, and most of the gardeners retire from the seasons with a real education about their community which they never could have picked up in their own backyards.

Since LISTEN started its gardens, people in the community who have never gardened before are drawn in. They come to LISTEN and ask how they can plant their vacant lots, and LISTEN will not only provide them with information but will also prepare their site and give them seeds and plants in return for labor or membership dues. One farmer provides manure to the sites in return for site preparation. LISTEN extends its services to about sixty of these home gardeners. These gardeners will get space in the greenhouse along with the community gardeners; they also use the root cellar to store their beets, carrots, and squash over the winter if they like. They can share in the lecture program when Marcia gets local extension agents to review the latest gardening techniques. LISTEN's gardening committee will also go into gardeners' homes and show them how to can, freeze, and dry their produce.

Marcia keeps emphasizing the fact that LISTEN belongs to the community. LISTEN members own the building and administer the programs through a board of directors. Marcia is not even on this board; she works for the LISTEN members. She is literally their employee. Her $90/week salary comes after all the other bills are paid from the combination of dues, contributions, fundraising, and subsidies. Clearly her heart is in the project. A lifetime of gardening has given her a center that is too strong to be buffeted by the scores of material failures that can happen in a grassroots organization; and because of her own love of gardening which she shares through the maintenance of LISTEN, the project has been enormously successful.

The garden program presently serves 175 families on three sites. These sites have been leased from private owners, in one case a church which will use the land eventually for expansion of their cemetery. Plots are 25 by 30 feet or 25 by 60. One plot is used as a community plot, the produce from which is distributed to persons in need. Last year the community plot netted $1500 worth of vegetables, while the average family plot produced about $300 worth. The community plot, while serving a survival need, is an educational device as well, demonstrating popular gardening methods.

There is a one-plot area set aside for teenagers and one for the elderly, so that they can help each other. But LISTEN has found that individual plots work out best because the majority of plotters cannot leave it up to a few more responsible workers to keep the garden going. The people seem to feel more privileged to be assigned an individual plot; although those without land of their own would appreciate any arrangement that allows them the chance to garden, sole responsibility for a single plot seems to make them happiest.

Marcia feels that the gardening program as well as the food-buying club has eliminated the frequency of malnutrition among Lebanon's poor. Her previous involvement in housing and welfare exposed her to a real malnutrition problem in small children. The city and county welfare departments work closely with LISTEN. Applicants for weekly $10 food slips are sent over to Marcia to sign up for garden space. The welfare officials tell the applicants that if they can't plant a garden, they don't get food slips. They have to bring back a LISTEN membership card and a plot assignment before they can get their food slip. Once these people start gardening, they are brought under the whole umbrella of LISTEN services, including the food-buying club, and Marcia reports that as a result, LISTEN has saved both city and county many dollars in food slips. LISTEN members are very happy that "at last Grafton County is waking up and not spending our tax dollars on those who won't help themselves."

In early March of 1977, Marcia had given out six in-kind service memberships in the last two months. That number is about average for a sixty day period. All of those were for applicants sent over by Grafton County Welfare to join LISTEN as a prerequisite to food slips. Some of these people cannot come up with the five dollar annual membership dues; they are glad to be able to work it off. Statistics on the number of these who go through the garden program to subsequently get off welfare have not been gathered, nor have they been gathered for those who were spared malnutrition because of LISTEN, but Marcia feels that the numbers of such cases are substantial. At this point in LISTEN's five-year life, it is enough that they are providing the possibility of cutting the welfare and malnutrition rates; for this alternative they present to low-income families, the community is grateful.

LISTEN presently has more applicants for the garden program than it can provide plots for. Even after the purchase of their permanent site, they will have to keep their leased sites. The permanent site will provide one hundred 25 by 25 foot plots in the summer of 1978. The three leased sites serve 175 families and applications have increased for the summer of 1977. With the hard winter, growing numbers will have to turn to gardening because of the soaring price of vegetables. LISTEN has had to turn away applicants for the 1977 season. All the sites are combinations of organics and chemical plots. Gardeners admit this is a real problem, but they feel that the program would be less popular if all sites weren't open to various combinations. LISTEN provides truckloads of cow manure to the sides of sites; then gardeners can shovel it on at their own discretion. Some prefer only chicken manure, some horse or pig, and some chemical fertilizers and pesticides. Marcia herself constantly keeps a tea barrel going of cow manure and water. The gardeners who use powdered insecticides use it only in periods of very little wind.

Gardeners who do infringe on the gardens of others, either by wandering insecticides or vagrant weed seeds, don't come back the next year. Problems on the LISTEN sites have ranged from vandalism of produce and manure tea to abandoned gardens. The site committee, composed of three members from each site, patrol their sites to find out what the problems are. They check on plot care and speak to people who are not weeding their plots. They guard plots that have been vandalized. They admonish gardeners who are not abiding by the set of regulations issued at enrollment time and, in some cases, ask gardeners to leave. They reassign abandoned gardens, according to the cut-off date given in the regulations, and supervise site preparations and clean-ups. June 15th is when abandoned plots get assigned to the waiting list. Before instituting this cut-off, LISTEN had an average of fifteen abandoned plots a year. This is a real waste when applicants outnumber plots.

And applicants come just by word of mouth from LISTEN members or because of the clever posters (Fig. 5) in supermarket windows around town. For the 1977 season, the program has had 200 to 250 families applying for space; the permanent site, when purchased, will not be ready for gardening until the summer of 1978, which means that leased land will have to be increased. The garden committee plans to hold onto its leased land year after year while they apply to the BOR or raise their own funds to secure enough permanent sites to accommodate all future applicants. They know that permanent sites are the only way to stabilize their community garden program. Presently, LISTEN's smallest gardening family is four; the more common nine to twelve member families cannot be accommodated by a 25 by 25 or 25 by 30 foot plot; they need double plots, which cannot be provided at present. So there are yet many citizens who need to be reached by LISTEN's services. The garden committee tries to discourage one and two-member units from applying for plots, which is a feat of diplomacy difficult to accomplish in a grassroots organization.

Half of the acreage of Lebanon airport belongs to the city, so the garden committee will go after that land for its next leased site. Other city projects have successfully gardened on airport lands, so the precedent has been set. Airport land is often beautiful to cultivate because it has been enriched with sod and is flat, with optimum exposure and drainage. It will be hard to obtain a lease on this land though, because the city of Lebanon has not been responsive to the gardening drive, according to LISTEN's garden committee. The city council has not come out to the sites to see the importance of the project in people's day to day existence; apparently it has allocated the seed funds for the purchase of the permanent site only under pressure—because it could not ignore the turnout of 200 LISTEN members at an open meeting. However, except for these occasional responses to LISTEN's concerted efforts as a political coalition, the city has virtually ignored the services

FIGURE 5

of LISTEN, according to its administrators. Thus the garden committee must supply all of its services to gardeners; they cannot count on annual truckloads of leaves or sludge from the sanitation department or on the machinery of the Highway department, as in other large city grassroots projects.

Thus the talents and resources of each individual LISTEN member are more important than ever because they must depend on each other for the organization's survival. A couple in their nineties provided LISTEN's manure for the 1977 gardening season in return for the garden committee's rototilling their home plot and providing seeds and seedlings. Another member has a big truck to haul the manure to the sites. Seven girls have the job of shoveling it onto the truck.

One of the members of the garden committee is in a wheelchair and must crawl to his 25 by 60 foot plot to work it. He pulls weeds on his belly and keeps the plot immaculate and flourishing. Another man was in a cast and had to crawl among his rows. Another who had to crawl was 82 during the last gardening season and kept the most beautiful garden on the site. The only special accommodation these gardeners get is a flat plot near the road so that they can get right out of their cars and crawl a short distance. Marcia maintains that LISTEN's greatest strength is its maintenance of the delicate balance between being there always at hand to help, and staying in the background with respect for the individual's capacities to help him or herself. The member of the garden committee in the wheelchair never misses a meeting, even though he has to pull himself up two flights of stairs on his knees and elbows to get there. The only help he needs is on the last step, which is a big one, and a friend to carry up his wheelchair. In another context, stories like this would be maudlin; among LISTEN members they are tales of pride because these gardeners who are dedicated enough to crawl among their peppers and tomatoes are people who, five years ago, were gardenless, disenfranchised of an activity that now must seem like a basic right, to grow one's own food. What were they doing with those long summer hours deprived of the soil? Probably watching daytime TV.

So now when they weed on their bellies or pull themselves up flights of stairs for garden meetings they have the pride of landed gentry rather than the pitiable mien of the deprived. Only the process culminating in self-forgetting that is the natural progression of gardening could achieve this kind of realism on the part of the handicapped and his or her observers. It is a process that is not articulated by the LISTEN gardeners but they all seem to be aware of something different that happens when they get their hands in the soil together. It is to the credit of LISTEN that this process is allowed to flourish quietly and instinctively within the delicate balance of reliability and distance that the garden committee maintains.

This committee makes all the decisions for the garden program, after getting feedback from the membership at open meetings. The committee appoints the three gardeners who form site committees from each site, then this committee appoints one of its members site coordinator. In the case of vandalism of gardens, the site committee must take the problem back to the garden committee, who then votes on what course to take with each individual case. Some vandalism is done by fellow workers; those cases are fairly clear-cut; the vandal is not allowed into the program the following year. In many other cases, vegetables are stolen at night or by drivers of cars with license plates from neighboring states, and there is virtually nothing to do in these cases but tighten the security around the site. No one is willing to stick around at night, although members of the site committee take care to drive by the sites in the evening. When a friend or neighbor of a gardener has been given permission to pick something from a plot, he or she must present a written note to the coordinator; before this regulation was instituted, vandals would simply tell onlookers that the proprietor told them to pick. The widespread occurrence of vandalism among community gardens is disappointing and the only drawback that can be legitimately pointed to again and again about the movement. Home gardeners are almost never bothered by this. The problem is due to the diverse groups attracted to multi-plot gardening rather than to the popularity or value of the vegetables to the vandals. No coordinator whom I have spoken with has come up with a solution. Chain-link fences do help; LISTEN's permanent site will have one, but fences don't discourage the vandals among the gardeners themselves.

LISTEN should be proud that this is its only problem. The fact that they cannot provide the necessary land for all applicants is a problem that other coordinators wish they had. The rapid growth of the program—from 5 families in the first year to 175 families in the fifth year—is evidence of the efficiency of the organization, the attractiveness of its five dollar per year cost, and the inherent respect for people and the earth that the program was built upon. When they move onto the permanent site, it will be a proving ground for the efficacy of permanent site legislation, and should reward gardeners by growing richer every season. After seeing the enthusiastic participation on leased sites, one can't help but feel that it is because of the security of permanence.

H.O.M.E.

CHAPTER 5

HOME is a successful cooperative set up as a non-profit corporation to help rural residents of Orland, Maine, avoid the welfare rut and become more self-sufficient. HOME (Homeworkers Organized for More Employment) was founded in order to stem the tide of small farmers selling out to big-time real estate developers. Now seven years old, it has touched the lives of more than 2,000 poor rural Mainers, providing them with markets for the products of their self-expression. In and around the modest farmhouse that is HOME's headquarters are workshops and retail stores for handicrafts, weaving, leatherwork, and pottery. There is a learning center for auto mechanics, wilderness survival, and raising crops for food and profit. Across the road is a farmer's market and the twenty-three outlying acres provide a haying operation for the livestock program as well as a community garden.

Members of the cooperative can take lessons in such crafts as pottery or weaving, then when they become proficient, sell their products through HOME's retail shops, some located in other areas of coastal Maine, and keep seventy percent of the selling price. Members' most valuable asset, the land, is put to new and constructive uses. Farmers are organized to grow corn cooperatively, which can bring them $1000 an acre, HOME keeping a small percentage of the profit for its building and staff costs. Livestock is kept at individual farms and rural homesteads and HOME acts as a center for information and resources on animal husbandry.

HOME's staff numbers somewhere in the thirties and each of them is paid the same weekly salary—$75. There are many volunteers who sometimes after years of volunteering manage to get funded positions. It is subsistence living but the staffers are dedicated to practicing what they preach to the outlying subsistence farmers: that there are elements of a rural lifestyle more valuable than money—fresh air, nutritious food, the slow rhythms of nature, fertile soil, and simplicity.

HOME was founded by three Carmelite nuns from a nearby monastery who decided to put their abundant energies derived from years of spiritual discipline to work. They wanted to help the neighboring poor hold onto a lifestyle they felt was basically superior to the alternative of selling out to the highest bidder and moving to the cities to join the urban poor. One of HOME's most valued and important resources is the education it provides farmers so that they eventually come to value the quality of their lives despite the lack of regular cash flow. This education in appreciation of quality is the closest HOME gets to theoretical knowledge. The teaching of specific skills that result in tangible products that can be marketed or exchanged for needed items is what is needed and what HOME provides. It seems exceptionally perceptive of the three founders to have seen that this was the gap that needed to be filled by such a cooperative, especially since the three founders weren't farmers themselves, but individuals steeped in a world of solitude and contemplation.

But this contemplative realm and the disciplines of austerity and solitude taken from it are perhaps what make the very concreteness of HOME's service so successful. For these disciplines provide the needed energy to keep HOME afloat as well as to provide a neutralizing of the daily frustrations or material failures any founder of a social service is bound to undergo. Another cleric involved in a similar project to put the means of food production and distribution into the hands of local consumers told me that a person who didn't put complete faith in the material world, who was grounded in a spiritual realm that transcended human attachments was less vulnerable to the frustration of material or human failure, and thus more likely to succeed in a venture such as HOME's that depends on so much cooperation.

The rural poor differ from the urban poor in that they have an alternative to paying rent and depending on others for their food. They can raise their own food because of the accessibility of garden and farming space. Unless the urban poor live in an area that has been invaded by the community garden movement, they still have to buy all their food. HOME came into existence to provide the rural poor with the initial capital and organization they needed to start to raise their own food and create their own livelihood. The craft outlets provided a market for skills already possessed and the education division taught new skills or made old ones more marketable. Then Down HOME Farming came into existence as a way for the rural poor to utilize their major resource, the land. They formed an association with Heifer Project International, a non-profit organization which provides livestock and assistance in animal husbandry throughout the world. In return, recipients of animals must pay one of the animal's offspring to Heifer International. This system has the same therapeutic effects that gardening does on underprivileged people: they have been given the responsibility for another life and thus shown that someone has faith in them to nurture and promote growth in some small organism. They know that they are depended on, and they accept that responsibility by learning animal husbandry; they also have the satisfaction of knowing that their payment will enable another person to make a new start.

Heifer Project has donated sheep, goats, pigs, cattle, and rabbits to HOME families, who use them to set up small milk businesses, provide themselves with meat, sell the wool to HOME's weaving shop, and create more breeding stock. To provide for these animals (sheep number about 150 and goats 65), Down

HOME Farming has purchased haying equipment, and with cooperative and volunteer labor and donated fields, processed about 4,000 bales in 1975. This didn't cover all the members who needed hay, however, and preparations were made to double the output in 1976. Unfortunately, it rained during a critical part of the summer of 1976, causing much of the doubled output to mold and the price to co-op members to rise from 25¢ per bale to 38¢. The moldy hay was used for mulch. The staff has had high hopes for the 1977 season because forty-one acres of fields were limed and manured in the fall of 1976 in preparation for great productivity. Even the increase in the baled price keeps the hay significantly below the going rate; members save significantly by being in the co-op. Members also hope to save on grains; a twelve-ton grain bin has been built and it is hoped that native-grown grains can be purchased to save money and encourage local agriculture.

HOME's education division has set up classes in animal husbandry, gardening and farming, and woodlot management. They have been well attended, with experts imported as guest speakers. High school credits are available for these courses and they are offered at no tuition fee. The free classes were instituted because of the realization that lack of regular cash flow is the biggest obstacle to self-sufficiency on the part of HOME members. To remedy this lack of ready cash, a revolving loan fund is being set up to lend money to members at *no* interest to provide materials for land improvement. The money would be paid back in four yearly installments.

The long-term vision of HOME's farm committee is that agriculture can be decentralized to reduce the waste of petroleum products that goes with large-scale centralized food processing; in the last sixty years the small farm has been virtually replaced by this wasteful system. The quality of life has suffered as a result of this centralization, and HOME wants to put the means of food production back into the hands of rural Mainers. Because its staff is willing to work at low-paying salaries and their overhead is kept as low as possible, HOME is able to provide the organizational structure that the small farmer has needed for all these years to survive. HOME encourages its farmers to use all available resources, such as seaweed in addition to manure for mulch and fertilizer, oysters, clams and fish from the coast, farm ponds for aquaculture, and animals to replace machinery. Farmers are encouraged to return to diversified agriculture rather than monoculture, which depletes the soil.

The co-op's founders believe that when farming was taken out of the hands of the small farmer and turned into a giant industry, the essential caring relationship between humans and the soil was obliterated. The consumer was to be pacified rather than pleased and the land was to be exploited rather than preserved because profit for its own sake had replaced the original motive of providing one's family and community with food. HOME farming provides a working model of an alternative to large-scale, centralized agriculture. It can serve many small autonomous farm units by coordinating and distributing funds, labor, services, and material resources, in a truly democratic and non-exploitive way because it is non-profit.

The newest aspect of Down HOME Farming is the community garden program. It is small but intimate because of the special relationship already created among its members by the co-op's unique service to the community. It provides a multi-plot site as well as a rototilling and free seed service to home gardening members. The program improved greatly as a result of a new director for the 1976 and 1977 seasons, a young woman who has years of agricultural expertise with Biodynamic leanings, who is humble enough to learn probably as much as she teaches or inspires. Rosa Lane came to HOME in 1975 and tightened up the administration of the garden program so that there was real improvement in satisfying gardener's needs in the 1976 season. Families of seven no longer gardened on space more suitable for three, but all families got the amount of space needed to grow a year-round vegetable supply for each member.

Because the site is only two and a half acres, it takes a lot of careful planning to give each family the option of a year-round food supply. A family of three, according to USDA figures, needs 3/10 to 3/20 acres to provide each member with an annual 400-600 pounds of vegetables, the recommended amount. All of the plots except one were completely used, yielding each family a year-round vegetable supply. Rosa and the planning committee see the site being gradually brought back to fertility with proper management. Having access to all the aged chicken manure they want, the co-op site crew fertilized it abundantly for the '75 and '76 seasons and in the fall of '76 limed it.

During much of her tenure in 1976 Rosa had to labor with the mistakes of her predecessor in the '75 season. One of these mistakes was the lack of enforcement of weeding regulations which resulted in only twenty-five percent of the site being weeded. Consequently, the infestation of '75's weed seeds was the main problem for gardeners of 1976, witch grass, lamb's quarters, and mustard having taken over the site.

Rosa had to tighten up the rules enforcing weeding and the planning committee introduced a bit of behavior modification to ensure both pest and weed control by sending a panel of judges at random times throughout the summer to reward the best kept plot with a $15 cash prize. In the summer of '76, fifty percent of the gardeners gained control of the weeds. The site has the advantage of being a permanent one and thus subject to cumulative progress, and with the tightening-up of the rules and sound land management, growing weed and pest control are assured.

All HOME's gardeners don't have land of their own to garden. Some are apartment dwellers, and one man tried to garden in his own yard only to find that the entire surface had been tarred-over at one time so that when he dug down he came to broken-up tar and gravel. Perhaps the reason most of the families utilize all of their plot space, thereby planning a year's food supply, is that they are all poor, and thus the chance to produce their own food is much more valuable than it is in suburban gardens, where I was hard put to find anyone growing a year-round supply. It is gratifying to see the optimum use being made out of a garden site. The program expanded to nine families for the '77 season, five of them or fifty-six percent returning from the '76 program. Since the site is wet on one side and has a road and other boundaries on the other sides, it cannot expand, so Rosa is submitting a funding proposal to start another site nearby, since it has been demonstrated that the families make optimum use of the present site.

Because of the cash flow problem cited earlier, the program was set up as a completely free chance to garden. But in the summer of 1976 a fee of five dollars was charged for rototilling expenses. It has risen to six dollars for '77 because the site is now plowed and harrowed in an attempt to reduce the weed population. The plow goes through early and exposes the weed's roots to the sun, then after they have had time to dry out and die, the site is harrowed. Rosa subscribes to the view that rototilling substantially reduces the earthworm population.

Last year a cover crop was planned for fall planting, but it turned out that gardeners were still harvesting root crops at the end of November for Thanksgiving, and then it snowed, so the site was not even cleared, much less plowed and planted. Site clean-up wasn't held until April. The garden is run differently from others in that the HOME crew does all the staking out and cleaning up; the gardeners volunteer for extra tasks like heaving rocks from the site, but as yet they are not required to do general site duties.

This is because the HOME program is still evolving to meet the needs of the specific population, the disenfranchised rural poor. The rules that apply for other populations don't apply here. There is not as much need for a tight organizational structure and guidelines because the population has been previously united under the umbrella of HOME's rural cooperative. There is an intimacy and trust already established among the membership. Rosa usually finds that when there is a job to be done, people turn out to volunteer their labor happily.

Garden policy is carried out more by suggestion than by rules. Emphasis is on organic methods but when it was discovered that natives would not give up running a little 10-10-10 down their potato furrows, the planning committee eliminated any non-pesticide rule from the guidelines. But miraculously by the summer of 1976, HOME's soft policy worked and natives discontinued even the 10-10-10 practice. No one used pesticides or chemical fertilizers. The educational emphasis on organics was totally effective, where rules or guidelines would have perhaps created some unnecessary sense of loss or resentment. Gardeners turned to organic methods of

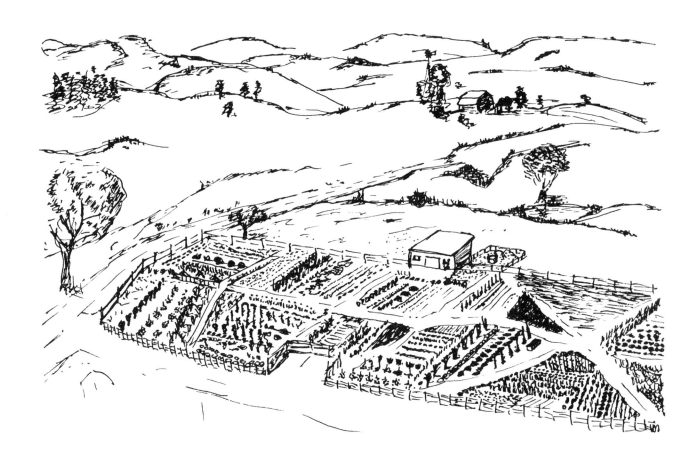

HOME'S VALLEY SITE

pest control such as planting a guard of nasturtiums or marigolds and putting wood
ashes on beetles.

HOME's soft policy of education rather than rules was instituted so that its programs would be as acceptable as possible to natives as well as new life stylers. The education department is up to date and provides a catchy blend of class time, field work, and visiting lecturers. Classes that attract gardeners are on natural pest control, crop rotation, and soil management. The cooperative extension agent gives numerous demonstrations of canning and freezing techniques and solar drying demonstrations have been given by an architect who designed his own solar drier. An expert on the economy of labor in the garden visited and laid out several sample plot plans that minimize gardening motion.

A demonstration plot that utilizes organic methods as a tacit example to plotters stands right behind the farm stand. This stand sits on the hill across the road from the white farmhouse that is HOME's headquarters. The hill commands a sweeping view of the valley where the community garden site sits. The valley was chosen because its soil is more fertile and moist than the hill's. Thus the demonstration plot is at a disadvantage, but sits on the hill because it provides the stand with leaf vegetables that aren't wilted and customers can even pick their own. This season Rosa will plant a demonstration plot right within the site to show the superior results of organic techniques. She will be planting in beds rather than rows to demonstrate optimum use of plot-space. Her own home garden is still in the planning stages since she lives on a wood lot which doesn't yet have space cleared, so she will harvest the produce from the demonstration plot.

HOME gardeners have an outlet for their excess produce in the farm-stand. HOME takes ten percent off the top of the selling price for electricity costs of running the stand. Since it is not a profit venture, members get ninety percent of what is sold. Fortunately, staffing the stand is no cost because a government-funded program sends teenagers to HOME in the summers, and these kids run the stand. Produce is sold by consignment, and most of the vegetables come from the local farmers, who can profit by saving the expense of their own roadside stand.

HOME's policy is to make each project as self-contained as possible. This is because the cooperative is for the members and the more participation the members have in each project, the more self-sufficient they will become. A volunteer co-ordinator from among the gardeners rather than someone from the staff is selected to oversee the site. This volunteer has to have technical knowledge of insect-control, companion planting, and optimum-yield planting, and has to make sure that everyone gets a fair share of the water supply in the frequent minor droughts of August.

Because of the community that HOME had created before the onset of the gardening program, advertising for enrollment is not necessary. The Social Services department distributes enrollment forms when it performs its daily outreach. The department services 200 families with everything from intensive counseling on marriage and family-planning to taking grandmother to the store to get groceries. The outreach worker connected eighty percent of the families with the enrollment form during her daily rounds in the spring of 1976, so that most of the enrollees came from the prior membership.

When the enrollment forms come in each year, it is a major job to make sensible arrangements of space to accommodate the specific number of members in each family. Families are now taking it upon themselves, after being exposed to the merits of crop rotation through HOME's education department, to keep plot plans from year to year and rotate their crops. Also each passing season gives them a better idea of what they must plant more of and what they have left over in the freezer or on the canning shelves by the following summer.

When Rosa first took over the garden program, she talked about blending some of the best aspects of both site plans that she had experienced in her gardening career—the communal layout and the separate plot plan. In the interests of sound land management, there could be common corn and potato patches among the separate plots, and there could be a community compost system, with a separate pile beside each plot or a single large area that gardeners would contribute their labor to as one of the general site duties. Now after observing how smoothly the separate plot-plan runs itself and how satisfied gardeners are with their yields as well as the individual preferences they have, she thinks that making these changes would be impractical. The gardeners don't have as much interest in corn and potatoes as they do in the more exotic plants like herbs. And most of them live over six miles away, making group composting inefficient.

Rosa came to HOME from a three-year immersion in Biodynamic farming, where she got first-hand knowledge of the pros and cons of the communal or single-plot layout. Her experience points up the reason so many communal projects fail.

"We first got together spontaneously, then we started intentionalizing the group. There were two elderly ladies on the farm, one of whom started farming Biodynamically when she was fifty years old and never stopped."

Being an avid student of Biodynamics, Rosa asked the woman if she could live on the premises and farm with her. There happened to be a turn-over of staff at that time, so she and five other young people were invited to join the two ladies to help them run the farm and to raise their own food entirely themselves. It seemed a perfect educational opportunity; besides the main farmhouse, there were three outlying houses for the crew's living quarters as well as a greenhouse and Biodynamic laboratory to measure the nutritive quality of the produce, providing the optimum environment to put Biodynamic theory to work.

52   The crew was responsible for the productive cultivation of five and a half acres. Two of these acres went to alfalfa and millet for goats (the two elderly proprietors drank only goat's milk). The remaining three and a half acres were planned according to the tastes and nutritional needs of the eight residents. Besides the three and a half acres, the farmers had resources for canning, freezing, and drying produce and herbs, as well as a root cellar.

Their position was not as enviable as it sounds. Farming is a seven-day-a-week dawn-to-dusk job, and unless one is willing to give one's entire life to it, the project will not be successful. Slowly the young people began to realize the totality of commitment needed, the same totality demanded of a new parent. But none of these kids had ever been a parent or anything else which demanded such vigilance, and the obliteration of all other interests was too Spartan for some.

Every day there would be an 8 A.M. meeting. One person was assigned for a week to survey the communal garden and come to each meeting with a list of specifics that had to be done that day. So each person was relied on heavily when his week to survey and manage came up. Not only were they gardening together but they were also practicing students of Biodynamics. This method includes attention to cosmic as well as organic forces, therefore sun, moon, and planetary and tidal phases as well as weather conditions must be considered. Thus the managing member had to explain the Biodynamic reasons for the week's duties in addition to clearly delineating what needed to be done. This meticulous care for the garden was in addition to other general duties like managing the animals, growing alfalfa and millet, and testing produce in the lab.

Lab testing was done according to two Biodynamic methods: capillary dynamics and chromatography. In both methods, extracted plant sap is registered on filter paper, and the resulting designs are indicative of nutritional content. In capillary dynamics, the filter paper is rolled into a cylinder and immersed in the sap. In chromatography the filter paper is placed on top of a dish of sap which evaporates onto the paper in different designs. Rosa said they would extract plant sap from their own produce and supermarket produce, and the difference was absolutely astounding, even to confirmed believers in Biodynamics. The lab was a great addition to the garden and is an idea for future coordinators and creators of community gardens, because gardeners can thus have more tangible and scientific evidence of the nutritional worth of their efforts.

Despite the technological encouragement provided by the lab on the farm, it became evident that some budding farmers were totally committed to the project and others weren't. Because the ones who weren't shared managerial duties, their lack of commitment lowered the efficiency and morale of the whole project. The group started talking about separating into individual plots for the following season, where only corn and potatoes would be shared communally. (Corn and potatoes are more practically grown in common patches because of the problems with hoeing potatoes plus potato bugs and raccoons.) If one member of the crew had been manager or leader all the way through the season, then those providing only labor could have shirked a bit without bringing the entire project down with them. The assumption that everyone has equal dedication and sense of responsibility to a job cannot be made of any group, much less a group that comes together spontaneously. Shades of the abortive tea-garden!

So although there was optimum vegetable production that first year, the following year the group split up into separate plots. Besides their own plots, the gardeners were responsible for helping the elderly ladies with their separate plot, too, along with the other chores of providing for the goats and testing vegetables. Often Rosa didn't get to her own plot till the moon was out. The combination of responsibility for the proprietors' plot and individual ones proved to be beyond the crew. The tendency was to feel obligation to the proprietors first and they would do everything else that had to be done before getting to their own food supply; often there just wasn't time to care for the individual plots. The communal plot afforded the farmers a chance to combine their obligations to the proprietors with their own food-raising, but the year's new separation proved to be more time-consuming than the combination. Raising two separate food supplies demanded a different breakdown of time and more organization than the group had foreseen.

Consequently the third year saw all food-raising done communally again, as in the first year. The crew ran into the same dilemma of some individuals willing to give one hundred percent of themselves to the good of the whole and others just not taking the same responsibilities. There seemed to be no solution to the problem of unequal abilities and interest. Rosa moved off the farm after the third year because the situation was becoming too ingrown for her own personal growth. It is hard to maintain a total commitment to the common good when everyone doesn't feel that way. Then personal growth does suffer because any disparity between individual goals and the common one is highlighted by unequal commitment.

After her communal experience, Rosa concludes that the individual plot method is much smoother because it incorporates the best of individualism with a group feeling that everyone is doing the same thing. HOME has provided the organizational center that brings members together in common projects, but they all go back to their individual homesteads or farms or plots to do things their own way. Each person reaps just what he or she sows and no less. However, if the dilemma of unequal commitment can be solved, as it has been for rare gardens like Ann Arbor's Ecology Garden by stringent regulations and the option of individual plots within the same site, the communal garden has the advantage that it can be steered in creative and innovative directions that a community garden can't. The crew at Rosa's Biodynamic farm would take an entire day to collect materials for the communal compost where long layers would be made out of seaweed, grass-clippings, dead leaves, manure, mulch-hay, garbage, etc. The layers broke down into light, black, sweet-smelling material that was the equivalent of the richest manure one could find. The only way this could be done at HOME's community site is to change the application process so that gardeners would commit themselves to a longer tenure than just one season, or to make a strict rule that a day's work on the compost is required for membership in the garden.

How good it would be to assign plots for more than one season so that one could see growing mounds of compost beside each plot year after year! With HOME's permanent site, this could easily become a reality. Already the garden attracts stable units, mostly nuclear families, although a few new life-stylers take part. HOME caters to the needs of the nuclear family, making it easier for them to garden by providing a day-care center on the hill where parents can drop off their kids on the way to the garden. For the kids that do accompany parents to the site, there is a corner with toy cars and trucks and castles of soil, where the children amuse themselves despite the lack of any formal recreation area or equipment. One can see from the way two AFDC mothers "govern" the gardening behavior of their children ranging in age from five to eighteen years that the nuclear family has an inherent hierarchy or pecking order that makes it a more efficient working unit than the intentional "family" of a communal garden.

At the end of each season there is an evaluation of the project which provides Rosa with valuable feedback for the next season's improvements. Individualizing of plot-space in '76 came from the feedback of the '75 season and the plowing and harrowing rather than rototilling plus the use of more intensive planting methods are a result of the '76 feedback. Families are now concerned with correcting their yields to make their favorite vegetables last all year. Rosa's French-intensive raised beds will thus be the perfect demonstration for the season. The families are getting to know themselves better as they delineate their likes and dislikes and draw up new plot plans that will assure that corn holds out in the freezer as long as carrots and that excess beans don't end up having to be thrown away to make room for the new stores. Tomato juice, dilled beans, and pickles were in abundance, and even lamb's quarters took up freezer space. Some of the gardeners in '76 got tired of destroying them and started experimenting with the weeds, finding that lamb's quarters steamed with butter and vinegar are a real delicacy.

This creative solution to the weed problem shows the high morale and good humour of HOME's gardeners. Somehow, making a bad situation into something light, humorous, and useful comes naturally to them; that might be because they are used to making the best of a low-income existence. Only one family experienced low morale on the project and that was because the plot was too large, a situation easily remedied. Rosa usually finds herself in the stimulating position of escalating curiosity each time a gardener has a question or problem. "I don't know, let's find out" goes a long way with the plotters, often leading to the fanning out by various members among many different sources and then coming back together to consult and share methods to achieve a common solution. Rosa is constantly learning with the gardeners and there seems to be a mutual awareness of spiritual growth concomitant with plant growth, giving the project an excitement that makes it stand out among community gardens in New England, despite its limited size.

Boston's Revival

In 1975, Boston's Mayor Kevin White allocated Community Development funds to expand the Parks and Recreation Department's Victory Garden program. Under the Revival program, unused city-owned vacant lots can be purchased by abutting homeowners with aid from the city in the form of improvements such as grading, the addition of topsoil and loam, and fencing. The program also expanded the Parks and Recreation Department's fourteen community garden sites to more than twice that number by 1977, taking applications from neighborhood groups with a nearby piece of vacant land. There was $11,000 to $13,000 available per site for improvements such as grading, fencing, and adding topsoil, loam, and water outlets. Each site is supposed to have eight inches of topsoil and loam by Revival standards. All neighborhoods have Little City Halls to process applications from neighborhood groups. The gardening group is responsible for its own coordination and organization, and for the division of the site into plots and their distribution. Gardeners provide their own tools. The Revival program also makes vacant lots available to individuals, issuing them seasonal permits to garden.

On the surface it sounds good, and when I toured the sites of Lower Dorchester and Roxbury, two of Boston's most economically depressed neighborhoods, gardeners were loath to complain because they know that despite the glaring mistakes of the program, they are still better off than they were before. They seem to try hard to see the positive aspects of the program, such as the fact that there was no attempt made before Revival to use the vacant lots for anything but dumps. Now with the strong chain-link fencing surrounding each site, the lots are refuse-free. However, the soil is in sad shape at many sites; weeds weren't even growing in the latter part of May because the soil was so depleted. Gardeners and coordinators at such sites reported that contractors had scraped off all the topsoil when they came to clear the sites of rubble and grade them. They replaced the topsoil with inadequate loam which appeared in many cases to be unscreened. Thus a lot that had once been overgrown with weeds would stand untouched, with no weeds at all, for a season after the contractors had graded it because the soil was so acid. It was impossible to dig down beneath the first three inches at such sites; as one coordinator put it, "the soil's like rubber. Your tool just bounces back at you."

Some of the sites were worse than others and there was a reason: all of the sites with rubbery soil where not even a weed would grow were cleared by the same contractor. This man got fourteen of the twenty-three city contracts during the 1976 growing season and, according to gardeners, botched every one of them. It is a mystery why the performance of the contractors wasn't monitored by the administration of Revival so that this particular contractor could have been replaced. As it was, he continually took the soil down to nothing, scraping all the topsoil off and replacing it with what appears to be unscreened loam, judging from the large amounts of small rocks.

Coordinator Marie Barrows' story of her site's preparation, a real comedy of errors, is typical of Revival contractors. Marie lives next door to the large all-black site on Savin Street in Dorchester; she is an avid gardener and has grown a splendid array of flowers and vegetables on her leased lot every summer for years. She is also loved and respected in her neighborhood and thus a perfect choice for co-ordinator. The site was scheduled to be ready by June 1976; it was even listed in promotional literature for Revival as having twenty active plots in 1976, but the contractor didn't even show up at the site until September, when the season was virtually over. The gardeners, all first-timers, had put their names in with Marie the previous spring and were raring to go. She hated to see their disappointment over the lost season.

But in September, she had no time for spilled milk; things really started jumping when the contractor came on the scene. First he confused the addresses and barrelled through Marie's carefully constructed fence with his bulldozer to scrape the perennials and topsoil off *her* garden. Before she got to him, he had rendered an entire section unplantable for the 1977 season, taking it down to the subsoil. There was no excuse for mistaking Marie's garden for a vacant lot, and the man was obviously a sloppy choice as a contractor. Marie is now taking him to small claims court after repeatedly asking him to replace her fence, to no avail.

In May 1977 four hopeful little six by six foot plots were huddled along an edge of the site where more workable soil was left than in the middle. They were planted by school children who had never gardened before. Although she was still painfully sensitive to her gardeners' possible disappointments, Marie had narrowed her own expectations after trying to break through the rubbery soil. The first thing she hit was a buried auto four inches under. She and the other gardeners spent the best days of their 1977 spring unearthing it piece by piece and getting it hauled away. How the contractor avoided it with his bulldozer is unfathomable.

She had to call a locksmith to install a new lock, because the contractor had fenced and locked the site and forgotten to give anyone the key, then subsequently lost it. But the gate had been applied with only one hinge, making the lock ineffective anyway so that at least Marie and her crew could get in to excavate the buried auto. It is hard to believe that this site's contractor was awarded fourteen of the city's twenty-three contracts in the first place, but then one gets doubly suspicious when Revival continued to award him contracts for the 1977 season, after Marie had reported all her site's mishaps in 1976. The administration sent no one out to check Marie's story and didn't seem concerned with the quality of work any of the contractors were doing. Because they saw no one in charge of quality control on their sites, gardeners lost respect for the program quickly.

Marie feels that if the Mayor had given her people three or four thousand dollars to fertilize and fence the area themselves, they would have had a better site. The eleven to thirteen thousand dollars that the city spent on site preparation bought Savin Street a site with a fancy fence and a pH level of four, where vegetables need a pH of six to seven. Marie and other gardeners maintain that the pH would be higher if the contractor had never come; the lot could have been rototilled from scratch and the consequent problems with weed seeds would be small compared to the present infertility. Observers of the site's progress say the city is perpetuating a cruel hoax, that getting people's hopes up and then disappointing them is intolerable for a depressed neighborhood.

But there are others who feel that urban gardeners are better off than they were before Revival. Bessie Barnes, coordinator of an all-black twenty-two plot site on Warwick Street in the Lower Dorchester-Roxbury area, has many problems with unkept promises or late dates but keeps stressing that she's not complaining because her would-be gardeners are better off than they were before there was any possibility of gardening. Bessie's site was supposed to be ready in May 1976, but the contractor didn't show up until September, so in May 1977 the twenty-two plots were all spoken for and had nearly a year's waiting list. People had planted and were nursing seedlings; retired people and children spent every day in the garden, while neighbors would stand around the perimeters leaning on the fence, fascinated at the new focus that had come into the neighborhood. The street and sidewalks were free of the usual litter and windowboxes were full of petunias and geraniums, while here and there a rose climbed a trellis up the brick walls of the housing project surrounding the site on three sides. Perhaps this site was so luxuriant because the majority of its gardeners were displaced Southerners who had always gardened, unlike Marie's people who didn't have the same kind of confidence.

There are two water outlets in the middle of the site. People hooked up a hose to each which would reach the entire edge of each half of the site, but right after the water was turned on by the Revival employee in charge of water mains, both of the outlets broke down. Gardeners hauled water from the project buildings to the site in plastic milk containers until an enterprising neighbor drilled into the side of the cement outlet and installed a faucet. Now one half of the garden can be reached by hose, and the other half still has to be watered by plastic pail. The

59

City Hall water official protested that both mains had been working when he had turned on the water, and that with only two employees to administer the entire Revival program, he didn't have time to get back to every water main that occasionally went awry. The people must take some responsibility for their own program, he said. A longer hose can't cost much. He had explained earlier that the reason not even a weed grew on many sites was because of this same attitude of letting City Hall do all the work on the part of the gardeners. He maintained that if the gardeners took more interest in the sites, there would be much more growing than not a single weed. The other administrator affirms that the gardeners shouldn't be babied.

This attitude combined with the initial give-away nature of the program, is the source of Revival's confusion and thus, perhaps, its sloppiness. City Hall has taken too much of the organizational responsibility for getting the gardens started so that the gardeners expect things to be taken care of during the entire season. If neighborhoods had been required to take responsibility for planning and funding the sites from the outset, they would have more of a stake in seeing the project through by their own efforts. The Revival administration could benefit from looking at the organization of other urban programs such as the LISTEN project, where the gardeners had to do everything from knocking on doors to collect site expenses to preparing and cleaning up their site from year to year. They take a great deal of pride in administering their program entirely themselves.

In this sense the administrators of the Revival program might have the right instincts when they say things like "Don't baby the gardeners." But somehow it wasn't made clear on the part of City Hall or the gardeners just how much responsibility each party was to take, and thus gardeners have assumed that things would be taken care of for them all through the season. If, as Marie would have preferred, the gardeners were given stringent funds to clear, fence, and fertilize their own site, they could have had more control over the outcome and felt a greater sense of responsibility. As it was, City Hall paid vast amounts of money to contractors and then had no system of quality control. The winning bidder was left to do the work alone and unchecked, and because the gardeners had no control over who was doing the work or how it was getting done, they had to stand by and watch mistakes being made, getting a low regard for City Hall in the process.

Some observers of the Revival program feel that the problem involves more than mere misunderstandings between City Hall and the gardeners. They feel that Revival was set up quickly as a political maneuver to win the Mayor more favorable publicity and future votes, in the course of which the "Mayor's contractor friends" allegedly line their pockets and the neighborhoods are left with the bitter residue of false hopes along with the remnants of a hasty attempt to hide urban

blight. From the many sites that will not now support even a weed and from reported admonitions from a Revival administrator to leave the contractors alone to do their own work rather than to check on them, it is easy to draw that conclusion.

But something less premeditated may account for the program's inadequacy. There are two administrators of the Revival program. One is in charge of furnishing water to all sites and thus has to visit each site to turn on the water mains at the beginning of the season. The other employee, who is in charge of awarding and administering site contracts, does not visit the sites even to survey a contractor's progress or results. The agency that was contracted to provide technical assistance to the program only sends people to do rototilling and collecting of soil samples; its administrator never goes to the sites. Unfortunately, unless an administrator or creator of a program keeps a personal plot on one of the project sites, the bureaucratic responsibilities and political ramifications of the program tend to separate him from the gardeners. The soil is the only level from which the pulse of urban gardening can be felt. Such projects as LISTEN and HOME, where the administrators garden alongside other participants, have a community spirit that seems to foster a stake in the mutual growth of plants and people. There is an atmosphere of encouragement and caring, whereas the Revival gardeners reflected an attitude of us and them—the disenfranchised versus City Hall.

Without this manual connection to the soil, the experience of the gardeners becomes theoretical to the administrators and creators of a program. An unfortunate pattern which organizers fall into is that despite their first year's tenure at a plot alongside other gardeners, they become fascinated by the new political leverage their position as creator of a fashionable community alternative gives them. They become more embroiled in the bureaucratic details of using this leverage to secure more funding or increase the scope and reputation of the project. The organizers of one of the first community garden projects in California found that branching out beyond gardening into solar and methane energy experiments brought more publicity and a greater possibility of grants for further exploration. Now, the energy of the garden's founders goes into campaigning for office at the city and state level on a kind of ecology ticket, and they don't have time for the gardens. We need more ecology-minded candidates running for office, but the truly successful garden projects are those whose founders don't desert them without filling a leadership vacuum.

The only existing bridge between Revival's administration and its gardeners is the Christian A. Herter Center for Human Ecology, contracted for the seasons of 1976 and 1977 to give technical assistance to the sites. Dedicated to "the renewal of natural resources, and to a process of relating parts to the whole—people to each other, to their institutions, and to their environment,"[1] the center has two

---

1. Pamphlet of Christian A. Herter Center.

primary goals: (1) to serve as a resource/catalyst for environmental education and action in the metropolitan Boston area; and (2) to promote the arts as a medium for building the community and developing the cultural life of the city.

Toward the goal of a resource for environmental education, the center established a community garden on its premises in 1975. Situated in the lush Metropolitan District Commission's twenty-seven acre Herter Park along the banks of the Charles River between Cambridge and Allston, the center's ultra-modern building serves as an office, an "Environmental Arts Design Studio," and a showplace for a permanent exhibition of memorabilia devoted to the life, work and ideas of Christian A. Herter, former Governor of Massachusetts and U.S. Secretary of State in the Eisenhower administration. The permanent and tireless occupant of the office since the Center's founding in 1974 is its president, Adele Herter Seronde, daughter of Christian Herter.

Adele Seronde is unequivocally committed to alleviating the plight of the poor and disenfranchised urban dweller; she believes deeply in the ideals of Jeffersonian democracy which, if pursued, would result in the only true aristocracy— that of merit rather than that of wealth or social background. As an accomplished artist herself, she wants to help the urban poor to attain the self-reliance inherent in any pursuit of excellence and full self-expression, be it in the arts or the soil. But self-reliance has always been a Republican concept that sits well with persons of privilege, the kind who dominate the Center's board of directors. Consequently, Adele has a hard time explaining her concept of "human ecology" to them. She walks a political tightrope between the urban poor and the inheritors of wealth and privilege, no mean feat.

She has trouble translating what she terms a "holistic" or "non-linear" view of the world to her board, since she, as an artist, probably has more direct experience of this kind of perception than business people ordinarily do. Adele's vision of "human ecology" acknowledges that we are not only irretrievably connected with all other life forms in the universe but also possessed of innate capacities that must find expression to provide wholeness and health. Visual imagination is to be encouraged; thus walls of housing projects surrounding urban gardens have plant-related murals.

An acceptance of the ambivalent nature of reality is another component of holistic perception that makes it easier for proponents of human ecology to tolerate the daily fluctuations in any social service project. What would be regarded as setbacks or ingratitude by a purely linear-minded observer would be merely another example of the continual interplay of opposites to the holistic mind. Thus, human ecologists appreciate what coordinator Bessie Barnes means when she says: "We need water; you tell 'em (City Hall) that. They said they'd fix that outlet and they haven't. Oh, I'm not complaining. This site was supposed to be ready June of 1976; it wasn't ready till after planting season—September of 1976. By now people are dyin' to get out there. We're still better off than we were before Revival." They know that things don't have to be either/or. A holistic-minded board would not categorize Bessie's reactions as ungrateful on the one hand or fawning on the other; they would be seen as two expressions of the same reality. The Oriental master Lao Tzu describes this acceptance of the unity of opposites beautifully:

> One who, preferring light,
> Prefers darkness also
> Is in himself an image of the world
> And, being an image of the world,
> Is continuously, endlessly
> The dwelling of creation.[2]

Adele Seronde is both a visionary and an organizer. She inspires and stimulates and then tries gamely to temper expectations by keeping pace with the details of making them work. Those details mainly revolve around the upkeep and layout of the large spaces available to the Center. Its building is the former Institute of Contemporary Art that didn't attract the expected crowds of culture-lovers because of its isolation in the large park. Despite the easy access from the well-traveled Soldiers Field Road and an ample parking area, the Institute wasn't patronized by occupants of the park, who come gratefully from the metropolitan furnaces every spring and summer to rest in the cool grass under the many tall shade trees along the banks of the Charles.

When the Institute of Contemporary Art became the Herter Center in 1974, Adele decided to turn the building's isolation into a positive attraction. She wanted to keep the building's artistic focus by continuing to use its vast open areas for exhibitions as well as classes, but she saw that Herter Park was filling its many seasonal occupants' need for communion with nature.

Adele combined the functions of the building and the park by providing a place to make a work of art with nature, in a community garden. Placed between the parking area and the building, the community garden was established to provide both a literal and symbolic transition between nature and the arts, as well as to alleviate high food costs for anyone who didn't have a garden site in their immediate neighborhood. Adele sees this combination as a necessity for a balanced life:

> What is the relation of the arts to urban gardening? From time immemorial they have been linked together as both healers and catalysts for human well-being; no civilization has been without appreciation of the intrinsic relationship between gardening and art,

2. Lao Tzu, *The Way of Life,* translated by Witter Bynner (New York: Capricorn Books, 1962), p. 42 (verse 28).

and their necessity as a setting, a conditioning for an integral life. They are central features in the mythologies and fairy stories of all peoples, they have surrounded kings and rulers, and meant the survival of serfs.[3]

The Herter community garden has forty-three plots, some only ten by fifteen feet to serve as many gardeners as possible. There is some room to expand, but that would be to the bank of the river, and it is feared that the proximity would be too tempting for the river rats, a problem not easily remedied by conventional fencing. It has been expanding for its three-year existence and each year there is a waiting list.

The garden has to be tightly run because there is nothing in common among the gardeners; plots are awarded on a first-come first-served basis, and gardeners come from many different areas of the city. A coordinator is chosen from among the gardeners, and she enforces rules such as the cut-off date for reassignment of untended plots. The garden has gone through the typical evolution of being casually administered in the first year, and then acquiring more and more rules after each season. It is a joy to see after viewing some inner city Revival sites with their rubber soil and untended but weedless emptiness. Each plot in the Herter Center is tiny, with every inch of space utilized. The layouts look meticulous and almost precious, as if each planter were fussy. This attention to detail gives an overall impression of great caring, as if every plotter's heart is in the layout. People don't just saunter casually down the rows. They work on tiptoe, as if the seedlings were sleeping babies.

Each plotter has a key to the well-fenced site, which keeps vandalism to a minimum. In one corner is a five-foot high group of slatted boxes for various stages of compost, which is turned and transferred continually. Three years ago the site was a literal rats' nest among intensive rubble; debris of this former state turn up here and there in the compost, but people who have worked there since the beginning regard the site as so vastly improved that the occasional sticks and stones are just reminders of how far they've come.

Expanding the focus of the Herter Center from a cultural and artistic one to an environmental one via the community garden proved to be a wise move for the financial health and future of the center, proving also that visions such as Adele's for the holistic wedding of gardening and the arts can be eminently practical. In 1976, largely because of the Herter Community Garden's success, the center was awarded a $25,000 contract to provide technical assistance to the Mayor's Revival program. Technical assistance consisted of rototilling every Revival site, taking soil samples of each site after it was readied by the contractors, and being available

3. Adele Seronde, *Report on the Effects of Urban Gardening in the Life of Today's Cities*, p. 3.

to the gardeners to answer questions. The Herter Center thus provided a liaison between the consumers of Revival and the administration at City Hall.

Jack Powers and John Allotson were employed by the center to provide technical assistance to the sites. Jack would do the rototilling and take soil samples while John, having a vast fund of technical gardening knowledge, would answer gardeners' questions. John was no longer assisting in the 1977 season, having given his energy to Boston Urban Gardening, or BUG, which is a grassroots association to promote urban gardening. But Jack Powers was still rototilling the sites for the 1977 season. He and his assistant Alberta McIlaney took me with them to collect soil samples from the sites.

"It's like they erased the blackboard," Jack said as he wheeled around the Dorchester neighborhoods he and Alberta had grown up in, in Alberta's worn out baby blue Rambler. "The housing project I lived in is gone, three schools are gone."

He recognized nothing except one old bar from his childhood—where they still have a "ban busing" sign. Even for a fulltime resident of these neighborhoods life must be confusing because housing projects are torn down and rebuilt so fast. Vacant lots come and go, either being occupied for a new project or suddenly appearing where an abandoned or burned-out building once stood. These lots are filled with rubble of every possible description, but even around the edges of ruined foundations there are usually places that can be salvaged for growing. Occasionally there would be a lone garden stuck out in the center of a surrounding sea of rubble—broken up concrete and rusted car parts—and the gardener had erected a make-shift fence out of junk—orange-crate sides and tin roof sheets, tied together by bits of old rope. Unsightly, but growing. This is rare though; most of the lots are left to go to weeds, which creep tenaciously over the rusted cars and concrete until the junk is entirely buried under a sea of vines. This jungle becomes so dense after a few years that no one ventures into it, and most of the vacant lots are truly abandoned in either the early stages of visible junk or the later mountains of dense foliage that lie in impenetrable and unnatural waves on a vast green sea. The Dorchester and Roxbury areas are filled with lots like these; it seems as if there is enough vacant land in these lots to feed all the inhabitants of both areas.

Having grown up in these neighborhoods, all solidly black or Puerto Rican, Jack knows the source of the constant renovations: the endless cycle of apathy, then hostility, then vandalism and looting, then abandonment of the looted buildings, then the tearing down and replacement with yet another impersonal hulk of a housing project in which the tenants have no stake.

"Neighborhoods fall apart because of transients; neighborhoods need people with a stake in them," Jack continued as we drove by corners of former haunts he kept feeling should still be there but were only recalled now by the street names. He said that every time he drives through there's been another wipe-out of an old hang-out. None of the schools that he attended remains. Driving through what should be old neighborhoods is disorienting for him, as if he no longer has any visible moorings. He maintains that to stop this destructive cyle of transients taking the buildings down with them as they leave the neighborhoods with the resulting disorientation causing more transience, "ten percent of every year's rent should go to tenant ownership, like condominiums."

Jack would gesture wildly in amazement at each renovation he encountered since the last time he had been down, and as we careened over half-gaping man-holes and pitted tar Alberta would pipe up from the back seat that her car's shocks weren't going to make it. Then she related her experience of driving through the old neighborhoods: "Some of these neighborhoods (in Roxbury) I wouldn't drive in alone, but in the truck with the rototiller I have no trouble." Neighbors know she is coming to fix up their garden sites, and it seems that the garden is neutral territory; there are no riots, no fights, and no hatred in the garden and Alberta still can't get over the miracle of it. Unexposed to the politics of the Revival program because she just joined Jack at the beginning of the 1977 season, Alberta sees mostly the positive aspects of the project—how the garden has reconciled groups that fight tooth and nail everywhere else. Driving around to see the gardens with a running commentary from two opposite perspectives—Jack's with the drawbacks of the Revival program, and Alberta's with the miracle of gardening—was a living lesson in reconciling the opposites, both of which were embodied and underscored in the presentations of the site coordinators I met.

Everywhere we went, Jack would establish instant rapport with gardeners and residents of the housing projects, showing how much it could help to have administrators of social services from the same neighborhoods as their constituents. The gardeners and coordinators would tell him their problems with the administration of Revival, displaying an us and them attitude which was not unwarranted, seeing that the administration never set foot on the sites. The employee in charge of water for the sites did turn up from time to time, as was mentioned earlier, but he maintained there was too much work for him to spend time at any one site. Jack seemed to be the man the gardeners trusted and confided in, and they were very clear about where he stood, that he was not part of City Hall.

But much as he tried to take the gardeners' concerns back to higher levels, he eventually found that his hands were tied because the Herter Center was politi-cally obligated to the Revival program who had given them a contract that would substantiate, if not prolong, their future. So all the criticisms that Jack brought back from the sites to the Herter administration were discouraged from going further. The few important ones that he managed to get to City Hall were stifled. The biggest and most obvious flaw in the program's organization was the lack of quality control of the contractor's work on the sites; Jack took this fact to the Revival awarder of contracts, who told him to leave the contractors alone because "they know what they're doing." Where did this implicit faith in the contractors come from?

Now in the hopes of remedying the situation, Jack is taking a survey of what contractors did which sites, as well as soil-testing the sites following contractor's work so that some responsibility as well as patterns of effectiveness can be attributed to certain contractors. The contractor whom Marie Barrows is taking to small claims court for bulldozing down her fence and scraping all the topsoil off her private garden has been linked with all the sites left in deplorable condition. The best Jack can do is submit his survey results to City Hall along with factual information such as pH levels, in the hope that the administration will avoid certain contractors next season. He will also have these facts at hand for any association that might succeed Revival.

Jack has continually gone to City Hall after being asked to rototill a site the contractor has just gotten through with, in preparation for planting. Often he is afraid of tilling such a site because the tiller throws up so many rocks. The administration orders him to do the best he can, and right before he drove us on our marathon trip to the garden sites, he had nearly quit the project in concern for his and the rototiller's safety. The administration has told him that his job is to rototill, not to ride herd on the contractors or report their results.

In fact, the Herter Center's job during the 1977 season is only to rototill each site and nothing else. Their contract was reduced from its 1976 level of $25,000 to $1600 for two months of rototilling in the 1977 season. This large cut could be for several reasons. Revival's budget suffered large cuts for the 1977 season and it could be that technical assistance was a luxury they could no longer afford. Jack feels that perhaps he and others affiliated with Herter told Revival administrators too many things they didn't want to hear and thus alienated themselves from another year's largesse. The Revival administrator in charge of water told me that City Hall had not been pleased with the job Herter had done in 1976, that all they had really given the program was a group of glossy slides and photographs of 1976 activity on the sites for City Hall's collection of Revival memorabilia. If this is true, then Herter's keeping their criticisms of Revival to themselves didn't seem to do any good anyway.

Whatever the cause, Jack got the word from City Hall that he was to rototill and keep his mouth shut—and he's rototilling up a storm, even extending his services to sites that aren't official Revival properties, such as a garden started on a vacant lot in lower Dorchester by an enterprising high school class spurred on by an environmentally concerned teacher. Jack took me to the site to bolster his theory that the Revival program has put too much money into the wrong services; that the money, and less of it, should go into providing good soil and technical

67

assistance only under the coordination of a community resident like Bessie or Marie who could generate neighborhood involvement. He feels that the gardeners would take care of fencing and clearing the area. This is in keeping with what coordinator Marie Barrows told me. She said that if the Mayor had given her and her crew of first-time gardeners $3000 or $4000 to clear, fence, and fertilize, that they would have done a more effective and caring job than the $11,000 contractors did.

The spontaneously organized high school garden proved that the gardeners could effectively clear and fence their own areas, and do a good job of it. Although the entire area isn't clear, as it would have been had it been bulldozed, there has been enough space made around the rubble to plant many vegetables, and the high-schoolers scrounged together their own fencing, not as fancy and uniform as Revival's chain-links, but effective. The area had been a huge garbage heap before the kids cleared it, and they stacked all the rubble and garbage out along the curb for the city trucks to pick up on their trash rounds. The trash wasn't taken for weeks and weeks, which caused more cynical speculation around the neighborhood about City Hall's commitment to urban gardening. Most likely the late trash pick-up was due to the usual inefficiency and confusion of an overworked and perhaps undermotivated big-city bureaucracy. But someone in the administration of Revival should know that if spontaneous sites like the high school project aren't taken under Revival's wing by being helped as much as possible— at least by having the same trash pick-up services that everyone else in the city has—neighborhoods will continue to be dominated by apathy.

The kids worked heroically under the leadership of their teacher and finally got the site cleared enough to plant. They couldn't provide any fertilizer, but healthy weeds had covered the rubble, so they knew they had a good chance of getting hardy vegetables growing anyway. They pieced together their own fencing to protect their investment, because by now they had a real stake in the space. Jack maintains that if the people have a part in the organization of their site as well as in its preparation, they will protect their investment by fencing and guarding against vandalism at their own expense. Jack was so turned on by the ingenuity and self-reliance of the kids that he offered to rototill the site for them. They agreed, but when Revival's contract awarder found out that he had rototilled an unofficial garden, she told him not to spend his time at unofficial sites.

Jack felt that though it was an unofficial site, its spirit was in keeping with the original purpose of the Revival program, to revive vacant land and put it back into use as well as putting the latent talents of city residents to work in an expression of beautification. Adele Seronde feels that the primary motivation behind community gardening is a spiritual hunger rather than a physical need to cut food cost. If there is any criticism to make of her contribution to the city's gardening program, it would probably be that she is too visionary and theoretical, not concrete enough, that she puts too much emphasis on intangibles such as spiritual needs rather than physical details. On the other hand, the Revival administration seems earth-bound to the most mundane degree in not rallying to the cause of such spontaneous and lively self-help projects as the high school garden, just because it is not an officially sanctioned site.

Jack Powers is trying to take the best of Adele's spiritual orientation and City Hall's physical one and combine them into a practical perspective from which to view the future of urban gardening. He is organizing various garden groups to incorporate under the umbrella of the already existing mechanism of Boston Urban Gardening (BUG) so that there will be a mobilized network to continue urban garden projects if the Revival program ceases. He knows from prior experience that the administration of such a network can only maintain contact with the people it serves by keeping its own hands in the soil alongside the gardeners. The Revival administration could take a lesson from the HOME and LISTEN projects and the city program in Los Angeles described in the next chapter. These administrations are headed by gardeners who maintain plots on the project's sites; they are not likely to be lured away from the soil by the temptations of power since gardening satisfies their basic spiritual or emotional needs. It is a way for them to remain integrated or centered amidst the pressures of conflicting demands. Jack Powers summed up the attitude necessary to an effective administration best when he said: "The act of gardening is an act of physical prayer; not euphoric, not meditative, but prayerful."

CHAPTER 7

Los Angeles Neighborhood Gardens and Farms

"It makes sense to begin to think in terms of a real urban agricultural model to be the first in the nation, and where better than in the City of Los Angeles, which once was a most productive center of agricultural products?" These are the words of Mark Casady, the dynamic creator and director of the city-wide community garden program established in March 1975. The Los Angeles Neighborhood Gardens and Farms program came out of Mayor Bradley's unique open-office policy where he listens directly to the concerns of citizens. Casady, an agronomist with a dream of putting the means of food production into the hands of the consumer, has now restored an area that once was orange groves and farms to a growing semblance of its former productivity.

As of October 1976, a little over a year after the creation of the program, Casady estimated that the city had as many as 3000 garden plots which provided food to 12,000 people. These plots were spread among twenty-five sites throughout the city, many of them on the rights-of-way for the city's power lines. There are 75,000 acres of unused land sitting beneath these power lines, and Casady had the unique inspiration of putting these acres to work. Now citizens garden beneath the lines, along the edges of freeways, on a three-acre strip at the airport, and in vacant lots. Even at that they are utilizing only a small portion of the several hundred thousand acres of vacant land in the city of Los Angeles.

Because of the endorsement of Mayor Bradley, the program utilizes all of the city's available resources. The Department of Public Works plows and discs land that needs it and also digs trenches when necessary for irrigation pipe. The Water and Power Department teaches classes in canning, freezing, and drying as well as nutrition and diet. The city provides free fertilizer, and seeds are furnished often from unexpected sources, so that in most cases gardeners have only to provide hard work, tools, and a few dollars per year for insurance and water. On one site, the Flood Control District is landscaping and improving the area with materials donated by the Department of Water and Power; they are building an access ramp, fencing and a barricade constructed of 4000 feet of poles at a total cost of $71,000. With this kind of spontaneous backing, the program has burgeoned across the city in the two years since its creation, saving families anywhere from $200 to $500 a year in food costs. Since gardeners harvest vegetables year-round, they now go to the store only for meat and dairy products.

Not only was Casady's dream totally endorsed by the city, but it is also an organic gardener's dream come true. The city-wide program is completely organic, which means that gardeners are keeping apace of the pest problem by city-sponsored education in what Casady refers to as biological agronomy. This eliminates the need for insecticides and chemical fertilizers which cause nitrate and nitrite pollution of underground water supplies and surface waters. Perhaps because of the air pollution and crowding of the city, Los Angeles citizens are hungry to get back to nature, and biological agronomy responds to that hunger. It is a unique city government that is in tune with its health-minded citizens enough to endorse an all-organic program. This is organics' most large-scale official endorsement, coming at a time of continued official discouragement from other sectors, and it makes Los Angeles the largest organic model of urban architecture in the United States. Mark Casady elaborates on the feasibility of growing wholesome food amidst urban environmental contaminants and touches on a typical official disclaimer of organics:

> Our research indicates that when optimum biological conditions exist in the soil, then plants are successful in defending themselves more easily from environmental contaminants. Biological systems include many defense mechanisms which chemical systems do not have. It is believed that within ten to twenty years all agriculture in the United States will turn from chemiculture to bioculture due to the superior defense against environmental contaminants, if for no other reason.

> Our experience with biological agronomy also indicates a superiority over chemical agronomy in terms of the nutritional value of the harvest. In particular, our biological systems approach to agronomy indicates a dramatic increase in protein content and vitamin and mineral values. This is particularly interesting in terms of current Food and Drug Administration attempts to discourage any claims that one or another approach to agronomy might produce a difference in the nutritional values of the harvest.[1]

Casady is an example of an enterprising visionary who created a job for himself in the process of starting the city-wide program. He was asked by Mayor Bradley to be a volunteer director of the program, to coordinate all of the city's resources to provide garden-farms. After he got it off the ground, the federal government provided funding through CETA to adapt food growing to an urban environment. The Los Angeles Community Adult Schools join with the CETA support to provide

1. Open letter to citizens of Los Angeles introducing Los Angeles Neighborhood Gardens and Farms Program, p. 3.

teachers at the gardening sites to give information on soil and plant science and insect control. CETA funding covers the cost of seeds and fertilizers in some cases, as well as the salaries of Casady and three other staff members.

Los Angeles Neighborhood Gardens and Farms has avoided the major pitfalls of the Boston Revival program, which we examined in the last chapter. The pitfalls were: (1) the administration's tendency to remove itself from the physical act of gardening as the program gains a foothold and some influence in the community; (2) a giveaway in which the gardeners give nothing to the program's inception and organization; (3) no quality control or monitoring of the services involved in site preparation.

The safeguard against the administration removing itself from the gardeners is built right into the organization of the Los Angeles project's staff, which is made up of eleven positions, the arrangement of which is shown in Figure 6.

The director is strictly accountable to the Mayor for the progress, effectiveness, and quality of the program. Written right into the director's job description is his responsibility for inspiring people into gardening action and, most importantly, it is stipulated that much of his time will be spent in the field on the sites promoting and doing agricultural work. Thus, the top of the organizational hierarchy is not removed from the soil.

The Scientific Group in the staff's structure is analogous to Boston's employment of the Christian Herter Center for technical assistance. The major difference, however, is that Christian Herter is an outside entity under contract for a certain period of time by the administration. Los Angeles' technical assistance group is a part of the administration itself, underscoring the fact that administration and proper soil management for long-range environmental health are inextricably united in a garden program. When the scientific group is out taking soil samples or doing research at the sites, there is no chance of an "us/them" attitude developing as in Boston, with Christian Herter the intermediary between gardeners and administration. If the scientific group's on-site research shows the need to change, the administration must respond. The group's on-site research is the vital link between soil and administration.

The two people in charge of the administrative/secretarial aspects of the program set up and maintain systems to direct and monitor field work. Again, the flow of paperwork is generated directly from site progress and problems.

The five field people represent the program in each of the five mayoral regions of the city. They go door to door in a potential site area to determine support for a community garden. They organize community meetings about the garden's progress, and check established sites frequently to report progress and problems back to the administrative staff. These people are different from site coordinators; coordinators are chosen by and from the participating neighbors in a garden project, to guarantee

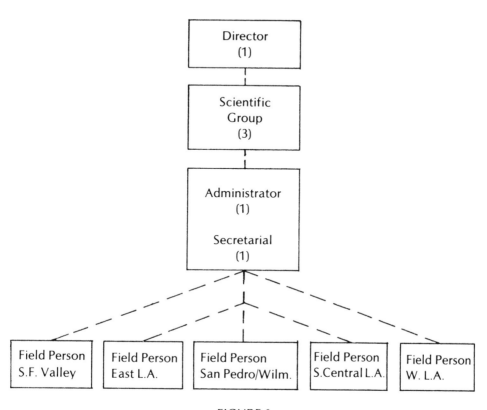

FIGURE 6

acceptance and rapport. From this level on down through the gardeners, the Los Angeles gardens are organized exactly the way the Boston ones are; neighbors get together, decide they want a garden, and notify the administration. The coordinator establishes a list of plotters and a waiting list if need be, and establishes plot layout, size, and allocations. The coordinator also determines rules for the particular site in accordance with administration priorities, such as no illegal plants and no selling of garden produce commercially. Fees are also set with the guidance of the administration.

Both the Boston and Los Angeles administrations are responsible for site preparation, but Los Angeles requires volunteer assistance from the gardeners, so that they have a responsibility not only for the organization of their particular site but also for its physical inception. The staff has the use of a rototiller, a tractor with a skip loader, a dump truck and a pick-up truck, which only the administrative staff is allowed to operate. If bulldozers or other heavy equipment are needed, the administration calls in another city department, such as the Department of Public Works. With the use of all the city's resources, it is unnecessary to hire contractors to do site preparation. Los Angeles Neighborhood Gardens and Farms seems to be doing very well without them, at a fraction of the cost of the Boston Revival program.

Los Angeles Neighborhood Gardens and Farms program is financed by federal money through the state Department of Parks and Recreation along with a grant from the City Bicentennial Committee. Four staff salaries are paid by CETA funds; the rest of the staff is volunteer. The total amount of funds available to the program in the spring and summer of 1976 was $30,000. Non-cash regular city support comes in the form of an office, secretary, and four city vehicles, as well as the particular instances of spontaneous support such as those mentioned earlier from the Department of Water and Power and the Flood Control District. Thirty thousand dollars is a small sum when compared to Revival's $11,000 to $13,000 per site.

Revival's expenses soar because of contracted site-preparation as well as the fancy chain-link fences around each site. Los Angeles can't afford such fencing and they find that chicken wire is adequate for their needs. Having site preparation done by staff and volunteer gardeners is a great savings with built-in quality control and the insurance of community spirit in the making of the garden. Their staff is rooted in the soil in its very conception, from the job descriptions to the hierarchical structure—the one on top does the most fieldwork. And all of this adds up to what community gardening is all about in the first place, truly low cost recreation.

Compost and fertilizer are provided each garden site by the administration, who obviously appreciate soil quality. Part of their educational program involves teaching gardeners how to make optimum use of organic waste materials from large scale producers plus their own household garbage to make top-quality compost. After rototilling, just before the seeds are planted, the staff works in a soil activator of a "liquid micro-organismic bio-culture whose purpose is to return to the soil the nutrients which are not all replaced by chemical means of fertilizing."[2] This is similar to the sludge program that many cities and suburbs are now experimenting with, dispensing the liquid fertilizer into lawns and gardens through hoses.

Director Casady has concocted a plot preparation recipe for the individual plotter to use on top of the staff's site preparation, which should yield the most dynamic vegetables west of the Mississippi:

CASADY'S ORGANIC PLOT

PREPARATION RECIPE

A Biological Systems Approach to Soil Management

Ingredients: One motivated gardener; one 225 sq. ft. plot (15′ by 15′); 50-100 lbs. composted chicken manure; 100-300 lbs. regular, homemade compost, or leaf mold, or horse manure, or steer manure; organic mineral complexes biological culture.

Mix: 100 to 300 lbs. of regular variety compost or leaf mould, horse manure, or steer manure into plot 6 to 12 inches deep. I have listed alternative materials in order of my own preference.

Add: 50 to 100 lbs. of composted chicken manure. This is rich, high nitrogen material, digested, ready and available plant food. This can be scratched into surface with a rake or cultivation.

Sprinkle: Organically bound primary, secondary and trace mineral supplement on surface. This can be scratched or lightly watered into plot.

Plant: Your garden.

Following
Germination: Innoculate the soil with beneficial soil microorganisms and watch it all grow.

Don't forget the weeding!

Arrangements for composted chicken manure, organically bound mineral supplements and beneficial soil microorganisms can be made through your Garden Captain. You will find the other materials at the nursery, horse stable, or dairy.

Casady has elevated gardening to soil science on a large city-wide scale and has put it across so that everyone can understand and accept it. The gardener has become a soil engineer, and there seems to be a real awareness that each gardener and each site is a model for a new kind of agriculture. There is an exciting frontier spirit about the project. Casady sums this unique approach up best in his delineation of "critical bio-mass," the core of the soil science taught and practiced by the gardeners:

Critical Bio-Mass is the sum total of soil life necessary to sustain optimum crop production. Physical Science (Nuclear Physics) gave us the concept of critical mass as the minimum amount of nuclear fuel necessary to achieve an atomic explosion. The new biological agronomy finds it useful to talk of *Critical Bio-Mass* as the threshold for a self-sustaining bio-system in the soil. The farmer/gardener becomes a bio-environmental

75

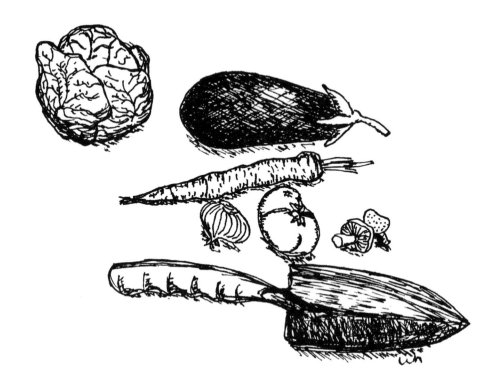

systems engineer. The farmer/gardener nurtures the soil bio-system, which in turn will nurture the crop.

Critical Bio-Mass is composed of a wide variety of living microorganisms and earth worms plus the environmental factors necessary to sustain this life: Air, water, soil, minerals, and organic matter in the form of digested protein, carbohydrate and fat. The successful farmer/gardener must understand how to blend these components for maximum crop production.

Chemiculture is often promoted as the *only* way for humankind to raise food and fibre. Organic alternatives are considered OK for backyard gardeners, but not applicable to the large scale needs of a whole population.

Metropolitan Neighborhood Gardens and Farms, Inc. (Metro Farm) is supporting research and development of a biological systems approach to soil management; a true, scientific alternative to chemiculture, for the gardener as well as the large scale farm.

Organizing a Community Garden

We have seen how a community garden can help a neighborhood spiritually, economically, and socially. Now how do we go about organizing one in the most efficient way, so that we don't dampen our inspiration with too much red tape? Gardens For All has pioneered in organizational methods, sifting out from their vast files of garden beginnings the major principles of organization and the timetable for their implementation. These principles are given in their manual entitled *A Guide to Community Garden Organization,* available at $2.00 from:

> Gardens For All, Inc.
> Bay and Harbor Roads
> P.O. Box 371
> Shelburne, Vermont 05482

These principles will be covered in this section, with individual variations that coordinators of several community projects have made in implementing each one. In this way, the gap between theory and actuality will not loom so large for future coordinators. There are seven basic principles or organizational steps that can be applied to formation of a community or communal-plot garden, the latter differing in site plan, land management, guidelines and regulations for gardeners. These differences will be presented following the details of the common steps, which are:

1. Finding a sponsor
2. Selecting a site
3. Recruiting a coordinator
4. Developing a site plan
5. Advertising and enrolling
6. Preparing and maintaining site
7. Encouraging communication

CHAPTER 8

Finding a Sponsor

At this beginning stage of the community garden, finding a sponsor should not be difficult. Existing gardens have already established a good reputation, providing evidence for potential sponsors of the low-cost/high-yield nature of the activity. The local city or town council is a good place to start searching out sponsorship if assurance of permanence is wanted; a committee or association of gardeners or a non-profit community welfare group can raise its own funds in addition to a grant from the city to purchase a site. If the city accepts the application for assistance, the U.S. Department of Interior's Bureau of Outdoor Recreation will match the city's appropriations to such a coalition fifty-fifty. This can be a time-consuming application process. A group in New Hampshire has been waiting over a year for the BOR to approve the matching of $15,000 appropriated them by their city to purchase garden acreage. While waiting for the other half of the funds, they have maintained a sophisticated garden program on leased land and have held the potential permanent site by obtaining an option to buy with what would otherwise be a down payment. When the funding is approved, they will purchase the land, then put in another proposal to the city for funds to improve the site with picnic tables, recreation facilities, a chain-link fence, roads around the site, and a parking lot. The city will then again go to the BOR to match funds.

A shorter route is to apply to the local park or recreation department. Many towns are endowed by private citizens with land and funds to make into parks or areas of conservation. There is a good case to be made for putting such lands to work agriculturally. One group in Massachusetts farms a large estate left to the town parks department. They grow hay because their upper-income suburb has lots of horses. The profits go back into the town coffers. They have over a hundred community garden plots, which are self-sustaining.

Recreation departments are sponsoring more and more community gardens because they have proven to be an exceptionally successful source of low-cost family recreation. Even the less sophisticated programs have naturally involved some playful interludes despite the lack of designated play area. Coordinators frequently tell the same story of children imitating their gardening elders by pulling rows and rows of carrots, mistaking them for weeds. At one garden the kids discovered an old overturned rowboat, abandoned among the weeds long ago. They managed to turn it over and fill it with sand; now it's a play garden.

Old town poor farms are another source of land for community gardens. Towns presumably would welcome proposals that would make profitable use of abandoned acreage, and the proposal can always include plans for potential revenue sources for the town, such as produce stands or haying operations. Community action sponsorship for low-income persons is another way to start a program, and application can be made to the Bureau of Outdoor Recreation or the Department of Agriculture's Cooperative Extension Services. Clubs and citizen groups can also be approached, as well as schools, churches, and businesses. If you are an employee in a larger corporation with some unused grassland as part of the grounds, you could make a good case for sponsorship of a garden where employees can work off competitive tensions during their lunch and coffee breaks.

Before any of these potential sources can be approached, one must go through the following steps to ensure an impressively detailed proposal:

A. Prepare a budget for the garden, recreation, and related areas.
B. Identify other possible sources of financial assistance with which the potential sponsor could join forces.
C. Determine a fee structure that would make the garden area self-supporting.
D. List possible fundraising activities to supplement original grant.
E. Line up and list sources of horticultural assistance (every Cooperative Extension Service will help by doing soil tests, etc.)
F. Develop an outline for land-use management to assure sponsor that the soil will be enriched and the land beautified.
G. Outline an education program if called for. Such an outline could include the teaching of gardening skills, nutrition, canning, freezing, and drying techniques, and various land-management alternatives for natural pest control such as crop-rotation and companion planting. The possible expansion into other areas such as a food co-op, cannery, research into alternate energy sources, etc., could be mentioned to show that gardening can be a vehicle to education and good citizenship.

The budget would consist of the cost of setting-up and preparing the site, the latter hopefully covered after the first year by plot fees. Site preparation would include the cost of water, the labor of spring and fall plowing, laying and repairing water pipes, tractor expenses, fertilizing, staking, and fencing plots, the cost of seed for cover crops, etc. This annual preparation cost one garden $1211 in 1976 for approximately 150 24 by 30 foot plots. This is the garden's sole cost because it has no recreation area to maintain. To set up a recreation area and related areas would include expenses of installing portable or permanent toilets, trash cans, playground equipment such as a sandbox, volleyball court, swings, or a jungle gym.

The following is a sample budget given in the Bureau of Outdoor Recreation's organizational booklet for a 100-plot site of approximately two and two-thirds acres—each plot twenty-five by thirty feet:

Site and Program Cost		Capital Improvement	
Plowing	$400	Storage shed	$200
Soil analysis	4	Picnic area	200
Site coordinator		Water installation	1000
(for a season)	850	Bulletin board	50
Hand tools	100	Maintenance equip.	700
Duplication	60		$2150
Postage	15		
Trash removal	50		
Water bill	90		
Educational material	20		
Insurance	30		
Ongoing costs	30		
Miscellaneous	100		
	$1749		

The budget for a sophisticated garden program could also include advertising expenses such as paper and printing costs for a newsletter, and a seasonal or year-round salary for a coordinator. Insurance against on-site accidents is optional; many sponsors don't feel the need for it.

Other possible sources of financial assistance would be especially appropriate to list when approaching private businesses, churches, clubs, or citizen groups as sponsors. These would have to be selected among organizations with related areas of concern such as aid to lower-income families, senior citizen services, and conservation maintenance.

The fee structure would depend on determination of current costs of maintaining the garden site from year to year. The garden mentioned above whose costs for site preparation were $1211 in 1976 charges a yearly fee of eight dollars per plot. This makes the garden virtually self-supporting because there are no expenses for recreational or other facilities. Another garden of about the same number of plots charges fifteen dollars per plot, but this program is part of the Youth Services project of a small town, and the initial funding is divided up among many different programs; thus every aspect of the garden program from fencing to education and paid coordination must be covered by the plot fees.

Income from the farm stand is a reliable supplement to the original grant, and since it has a proven record, is a good possible activity to list in a proposal. The gardeners can either be required to donate a certain amount of produce to the stand weekly, or a separate demonstration plot can be devoted exclusively to the farm stand, at the same time being used as a tacit standard of good gardening techniques for beginning gardeners to emulate. One garden has both a farm stand and, because of its proximity to the main road, several "picking patches," where customers come from the inner city to pick their own fresh produce. There are any number of proven fundraising schemes that can be presented in the proposal package—from spring garage sales to fall harvest festivals.

Sources of horticultural assistance are the local cooperative extension service, a nearby university or agricultural college (students of horticulture can sometimes help on a work-study basis), local garden clubs, and conservation groups. The extension service will test the soil year after year once a garden is established. One program was lucky enough to have a work-study student in soil science who got carried away and tested *every one* of the 135 plots; the coordinator then made up a color-coded chart showing the pH level of every plot and posted it in the central meeting barn. This was a real help to the gardeners since they chose their plots every year.

The outline for land-use management should include potential plot layouts, with walkways between plots and designated areas for single-crop patches such as corn and potatoes. Corn and other tall plants such as sunflowers in individual plots can shade adjoining plots, thus in some layouts it is more practical to plant it in a common patch. A common patch of potatoes assures the possibility of a long-range plan of crop rotation to build up the soil and provide natural pest resistance. If the proposal is for a communal garden, a complete plan for companion planting for insect control can be given. Crop rotation is assured in a single-plot garden.

The education program can be presented in an exciting way, with mention of the possible expansion into alternate energy sources as a natural evolution of the gardening process. Expert gardeners representing different methods or specialties can be listed as possible visitors. Representatives from gardens that have developed localization of food sources through co-ops that buy from local producers or central canneries can be listed. One group has advanced from the teaching of canning techniques to the installation of a central cannery for all its gardeners. Gardens that have expanded in such innovative directions are inspirational and can serve to excite the sponsor about far-ranging ecological ramifications of the gardening movement.

Complete coverage of all of these steps might not be possible before one has some experience with a community garden, but it is important in writing a funding proposal to include as many relevant details as possible without cluttering the thrust of the application. Specifics assure the potential sponsor that much thought has been put into the proposed program, and this forethought is especially appreciated in the area of the budget and fee structure. It is a good idea also to include an introductory paragraph on why and how a community garden would serve the specific locale: the economic value, the social benefits of improved community relations, and, depending on the sponsoring institution, the spiritual and therapeutic dividends.

CHAPTER 9

Selecting a Site

Possible sites could be included in the application for sponsorship, especially when churches or businesses which already have suitable areas of unused land are approached. But if an obvious site hasn't already presented itself, or if several alternatives cited as part of the funding package have yet to be sifted through, selecting a site will be the next step. Though it is not practical to go around soil-testing all possible sites, a few obvious requirements are that much of the site get equal exposure to lots of sun, that there be good drainage and no possibility of flooding, that there be enough space so the projected population can grow a season's vegetable supply with some left to preserve for the winter, that there be a nearby water source, and that there be good accessibility and parking. Tilth and pH can be built up. Most gardens report that in the beginning the soil had to be limed and fertilized intensively to bring it back to productivity, but then cover crops or yearly town leaves or manure plowed in keeps it rich.

Weeds aren't as much of a problem as many people believe. The best a co-ordinator can do is to try to avoid sites with tough weeds like quack grass and Canada thistle, plow all material under during initial preparation, and then leave the weed control to individual gardeners to tackle plot by plot. One coordinator advises gardeners to dig a deep hole in the corner of every plot, put all weeds into it and sprinkle it with a layer of soil; he claims that as long as they are covered with soil, the weeds will decompose into compost in twenty days. He doesn't assign the same negativity to weeds that other coordinators do because he believes that weeds' roots run deeper, thus bringing up nutrients that other plants can't reach. Another garden finds that lamb's quarters, an all too common weed, are great steamed.

If the garden is located on a main road, some coordinators plug right into a nearby hydrant, spreading the water to all boundaries of the site by pipe. Most towns are generous with their hydrants, and plastic pipe is not hard to lay—outlets can even be left at the garden site through the winter along with boundary stakes. In deciding on whether a particular site is going to accommodate the projected number of families, it is good to calculate plots of 25 by 30 feet, thus giving each plotter plenty of room. Then the standing water outlets are positioned along the width of about every three plots, making irrigation convenient. This convenience matters a great deal. Rachel Kaplan found that the response of separate plotters could not even be measured objectively compared to the communal or home gardeners in her study because the inconvenience of irrigation made their gardening experience less than satisfying.[1] It is worth it to spend extra time to surface the plastic pipe at many outlets. A few gardeners disgruntled by long treks with pails of water can dampen the whole spirit of the project.

When the site has been selected, a formal land-use commitment must be obtained. If the owner is not readily known, the city planning department, local tax assessor, or even the regional office of the Bureau of Outdoor Recreation (for federally-owned lands) have data on ownership. The land-use commitment can be a simple written lease, provided by the owner. It is a good idea, from the owner's standpoint, to get insurance against injury of gardeners while on the premises, but a good many towns which own garden sites have not found this necessary. Some have a clause in their garden agreement that pledges the gardener not to sue if injured. Several sponsors who are five and six years into the project without insurance recognize the need for it and plan to make sure they are covered in years to come. [My interviews yielded no stories of injuries or suits.]

1. Kaplan, op. cit., pp. 150, 151.

CHAPTER 10

Recruiting a Coordinator

After the sponsorship and site are formally obtained, a coordinator must be recruited to direct the program and participate in the last four steps of developing the garden. Whether to pay the coordinator a salary or ask for a volunteer should have been decided before step number one so that a sponsor would agree to cover the cost of the salary. I strongly urge that a coordinator be paid. Volunteerism is often subscribed to in a surrounding atmosphere of hope, idealism, and false expectation. As time goes on, these hopes are often shattered by the actual performance and attitude of the volunteer and the project becomes permeated with bad feeling. A volunteer is necessarily committed to another job which must take precedence, either for financial reasons or family duty as in the case of homemakers. A volunteer is going to feel exploited, and rightly so, if asked to do more than he or she *elects* to do. Most volunteers complain of a lack of direction; since they are giving their time, co-workers are inhibited about making demands on them. "Oh, just look around and see what needs to be done" is too often the response to a volunteer on the first day of work. There is a healthy feeling of contract in the receiving of money for a job—one feels one must earn it, give something back for it, and this something is easier to define with a salaried coordinator. The value of a salary is in the detailed and concrete quality of the demands on the employee and his or her responding effort.

A monthly checklist of activities and tasks for the garden coordinator can be found in the appendix and shows that the job of organizing a sophisticated program can warrant a year-round salary. Branching out into solar dehydration or the installation of a cannery or a food co-op can add to a salaried coordinator's year-round obligations.

Here are the seasonal duties which a coordinator of a 75- to 100-plot site should be responsible for.[1]

Working Conditions
Twenty hours a week - primarily evenings and weekends

86   1. Bureau of Outdoor Recreation, *Recreational Community Gardening,* p. 9.

Duties

Establish liaison with cooperative extension agent or other qualified horticultural expert and plan garden education program. Work with volunteers and staff on site and program development. Clear all projects for clean-up, physical development, and special programs with appropriate agency.

Site Responsibilities

1. Map site, stake, and assign plots
2. Develop and maintain:
    a. Picnic area
    b. Play area
    c. Rock piles
    d. Composting system
    e. Trash removal system
    f. Overall site clean-up
    g. Bulletin boards — current information
    h. System for use of water
3. Plant and maintain a demonstration garden
4. Maintain tools and other equipment

Program Responsibilities

1. Establish a volunteer site committee
2. Develop guidelines and rules for use of site with site committee and appropriate agency.
3. Organize:
    a. Garden tours
    b. Picnics
    c. Educational talks
    d. Harvest party
4. Write newsletter
5. Maintain written and pictorial record of site activities
6. Be available on a regular basis to disseminate garden information, loan out and care for project tools and recreation equipment, conduct routine site maintenance, keep lists of all volunteers and resources, and act as liaison for people needing assistance.
7. Supervise and coordinate use of site and any buildings

It is also a real accomplishment to *create* a job in an area of economic alternatives to the present food production and marketing system, which a community garden certainly is. That a person committed to such alternatives can make a living at helping to create and maintain such a project is further proof of its viability. Volunteer coordinators are much quicker to grow disgruntled with such alternatives;

87

paid coordinators are naturally expansive and their projects grow with them. One program coordinator, salaried by Federal Community Action funds, has developed his community garden into many small self-sustaining neighborhoods, each one growing the major portion of its food supply and supporting its project with farm stands. Being in Southern California, they have the advantage of a continuous growing season.

Having a salaried coordinator doesn't preclude the benefits of volunteer labor. Many successful gardens develop a core of gardeners who turn into volunteer organizers; however, having a salary to offer assures that at least one member of this core group is as highly qualified as the sponsor desires. The coordinator should be prepared, in the course of a growing season, to answer questions about new techniques and methods, such as French Intensive and Bio-dynamic modes of organic gardening, should know principles of companion planting and successive cropping as well as details of soil fertility, disease and insect control, composting, and land management. Implementation of a good land-management program at the beginning of a garden project can spare gardeners many future diseased plants, so a coordinator should be capable of working out a land-use program—a difficult thing for a community garden because the separate plot plan discourages easy crop rotation. But a qualified coordinator can map out a long-term crop rotation policy in the beginning either by having common patches of several vegetables or by requiring each plotter to keep detailed plot plans from year to year.

So a coordinator should know quite a bit about gardening and should possess the curiosity necessary to investigate new cultural trends (such as alternate energy sources to use in connection with gardening) as well as new techniques. A coordinator should have some managerial skills as well as organizational expertise. He or she should also be tactful and patient despite this expertise because the separate plot situation means that the coordinator must know how to persuasively suggest improvements to gardeners but stop short of pushing anything. Often it helps if a coordinator isn't previously committed to any one gardening philosophy. The coordinators I interviewed who *are* so committed are more interesting to talk with, but their previous alliance to certain set principles makes them much more frustrated when gardeners don't adhere to them. The most impressive coordinators I've interviewed, however, *are* committed to some gardening philosophy, such as Bio-dynamics, that brings them to the job with inspired ideals, *and* they have learned patience and respect for the individuality of each gardener's separate sensibility and pace on the job. They possess a rare combination of inspiration and humility. Often these coordinators have a separate space of their own to express the principles of their commitment, such as a demonstration garden alongside the rest of the plots, that is much more persuasive than words. Or a philosophy can be expressed in a newsletter for the garden project that is circulated all year to keep the garden spirit alive from season to season. One coordinator has two columns in the local paper—one to explain the latest practical methods and the other to air his ideals and philosophy. This outlet permits him to have the patience on the garden site to let the gardeners struggle along their own paths and, best of all, allows him to learn from them.

For the hiring or recruiting process, a job description can be written up from the timetable in the appendix and from the list of coordinator's obligations on page 87. The sponsor or garden committee can amend this according to their specific needs. The initiation for the coordinator can consist of walks over the land with the garden committee and/or the local cooperative extension agent or a professor of horticulture at a local college. These walks can be the basis for a land-management plan before the season begins and can continue throughout the season for disease and pest control as well as gardener's questions that the coordinator couldn't answer on the spot. A walk over the site with an expert is worth a thousand words and addresses the particularity of the site, something a classroom or lecture situation can't do as well.

The coordinator who brings curiosity to the job will be expanding his education daily and will eagerly bring in experts on any new breakthrough in garden techniques or food preservation. A coordinator with curiosity will naturally unfold a varied and continuing education program for the gardeners. Gardening expertise, an ability to get along with people, and a hearty curiosity are the most important qualifications for a coordinator. Innate curiosity can take the place of a formal training program although the pre-season walks over the site with the cooperative extension agent are invaluable.

In many cases, garden coordinators are also committed to ideals such as equal distribution of the planet's resources, so that they don't require large salaries. They are used to getting along on very little. One coordinator I interviewed is very happy in a year-round coordinating position which pays $75 per week. A good range to present in a budget proposal to potential sponsors is between $5000 and $8000 a year, or for a seasonal commitment, $100 to $150 per week. In another program, two assistants to the coordinator split a year-round $100/week salary from the town and feel privileged to be paid for helping the community. In some cases, the entire project has been the coordinator's idea, so in addition to naming his own salary figure, he selects a site and sponsor. In these cases, a person has been assertive and innovative enough to create his own job, consistent with previously held ecological principles. And a self-created job is usually the most satisfying kind to have, so these individuals bring a special sense of accomplishment and contentment to the project.

CHAPTER 11

Developing a Site Plan

Development of a site plan is the first major responsibility of a coordinator who hasn't been in on the initiation of the entire project. A land-management program which determines such things as whether to plow in the fall, plant a winter cover-crop, have gardeners control disease by destroying individual diseased plants or rotating crops, should already have been established by the sponsor's garden committee or horticultural experts if the coordinator has not been in the picture yet. A site-plan establishes plot size and layout with walkways and aisles, and storage, recreation, rest, and expansion areas.

The standard plot size is 25 by 30 feet, sometimes 30 by 30 feet. If families want to grow a year-round vegetable supply (each member should eat between 400 to 600 pounds of vegetables a year),[1] they can use multiples of the basic standard plot. Sample plots for different regions have been provided in the appendix.

Most community gardens don't have many "survival gardeners," or growers of year-round supplies, so planners determine their basic plot size according to the recreational and seasonal needs of the average gardener. Large plots discourage beginning gardeners, resulting in abandonment or weed problems.

A few sample site layouts follow (Figs. 7-8); these are sites of typical community gardens and one can see that they are not as highly evolved as the layout of the typical English Leisure Garden, shown on page 18. Some gardens limit their plot space by providing a walkway around the boundaries of each plot. These walkways are sometimes lined in woodchips, sometimes mown grass, and sometimes just packed soil. There are usually fences around the outer boundaries of the entire plot area, though some gardens that have been going for six or seven years have dispensed with fencing altogether because woodchucks still manage to tunnel under them. One of these gardens is fortuitously situated right across the main road from the town police station, thereby discouraging vandalism, a bigger problem for community gardens than woodchucks.

Walkways should be about four feet wide, to allow wheelchairs, carts, and wheelbarrows access as well as gardeners. Aisles around every individual plot seem

1. W.H. Erhardt, *Home Vegetable Gardening,* Cooperative Extension Bulletin 544, (Revised), p. 2.

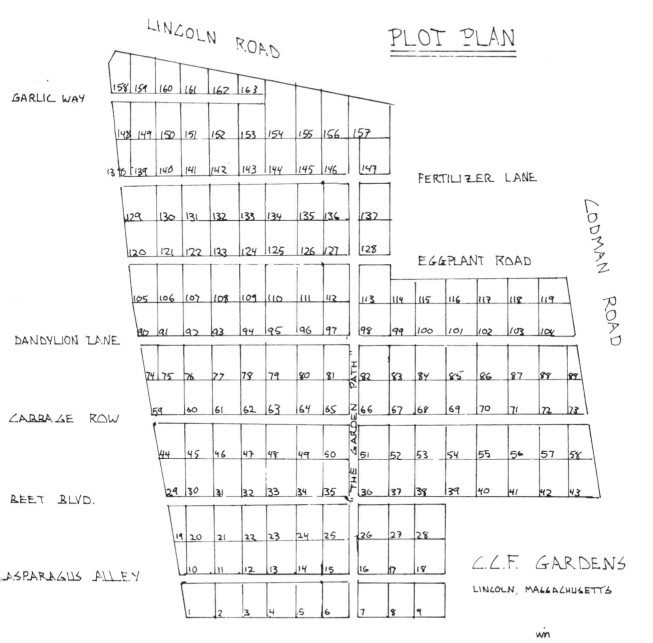

FIGURE 7   CODMAN COMMUNITY FARMS GARDEN   **91**

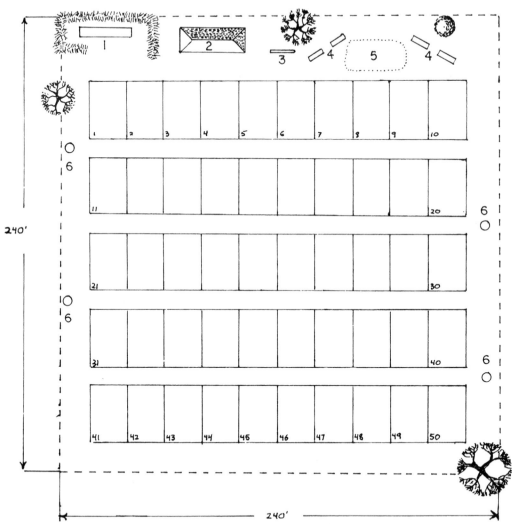

SITE PLAN   ABOUT 1⅓ ACRES

LEGEND

1 COMPOST
2 TOOL SHED
3 BULLETIN BOA
4 BENCHES
5 PLAY AREA
6 TRASH CANS

240'

240'

FIGURE 8   BOR LAYOUT

unnecessary, especially upon study of some of the layouts in Figures 7 and 8. Such layouts should be drawn up and posted in a central location by coordinators, with numbered plots so that gardeners can get a feel for where they will be located in the total site picture when they choose or are assigned a plot.

It is pleasing to imagine gardens with picnic areas, volleyball courts, portable toilets, tool houses, and a central meeting place, but until secure permanent site legislation is enacted, such embellishments are only found in the most established and financially secure programs. Most gardens have the bare minimum—a toilet, trash cans, and perhaps a few picnic tables. One garden parks a trailer close by the plots and all the trash is thrown directly into the vehicle which then gets hauled to the dump when full. Other gardens have old barns or storage sheds or milkhouses already on the site that can provide tool storage and perhaps a place to install a toilet if one isn't there already. Many gardens have gardeners come and leave with their own tools. The outlying areas seem to be the last developed, the main energy of a beginning garden being devoted to plot arrangement.

CHAPTER 12

Advertising and Enrolling

Before advertising, the coordinator or garden committee must determine priorities for the garden site: whether it is primarily for educational or recreational purposes. Along with the enrollment forms should go a list of guidelines and regulations for plotters, and a general statement of purpose to explain these restrictions. Several programs started out with minimal restrictions and had to add them as they expanded. To draft guidelines before a program is underway requires thorough examination by the coordinator, sponsor, and garden committee as to what they want the garden to be. Pages 96-102 show some sample enrollment forms with guidelines. These necessitate a real commitment from the gardener before he or she is assigned a plot. In most cases, the guidelines and enrollment forms can be combined on the front and back of one sheet.

Guidelines should give rental fees for plots and the times of access to the site. If possible, there should be an indication that free plots are available to those who can't afford the plot fee. The restrictions depend on the project's priorities. It is easier if it can be determined that the garden will be completely organic; combinations of organic areas and pesticide areas are much harder to administer and enforce. If a strictly organic policy cannot be decided upon, restrictions on any particular pesticide that the garden committee or coordinator has deemed more harmful than others should be clearly spelled out. Certain areas on a plot plan should be designated as organic only, and if a plot plan is not available, it should be made clear that certain areas will be so designated before plots are chosen or assigned. One coordinator found it virtually impossible, even with ongoing education during the gardening season, to wean oldtime Mainers from a little 10-10-10 (10% nitrogen, 10% phosphorus, 10% potassium) under potato plants. Their habits were too ingrained.

There should be a restriction against planting of June-bearing perennial fruits and vegetables, unless special perennial plots are provided. Most beginning garden projects just state "no perennials." The planting of excessively tall plants which could shade neighboring plots is not usually a problem, but a restriction against this should be included. Bringing unleashed pets can be a real problem—a coordinator's obedient dog could be a good garden mascot if it didn't set a bad precedent. In most cases it does and other gardeners get casual about bringing their curious pets.

There's nothing more maddening than a friendly dog lying down on a row of lettuce or digging up the carrots.

Driving on the garden site, believe it or not, has occurred in gardens close to a main road. One coordinator has problems with teenage friends of gardeners riding their motorcycles through the squash patch; this is because the kids were allowed in the first place to ride their motorcycles around the outlying areas of the plots. There must be a clear injunction against vehicles on the site, or they should be limited to the parking area. The planting of poisonous or illegal plants must be another forbidden item; marijuana enthusiasts will have to continue growing their dope under lights in closets or in pots on their roofs.

Abandonment of plots and low turn-outs at fall clean-ups have plagued community garden coordinators at nearly every project I visited except the very small ones. One coordinator included in the guidelines and restrictions the date that un-attended plots will be reassigned. This is June 15 in her region of New England, but it could be earlier further south. In every large project there are bound to be beginners who plan a garden larger than they are willing to care for. The plot re-assignment policy seems to work well; the date could be accompanied by an ex-planation with examples from the past when there was no such policy. Many younger group gardeners are dead set against anything that smacks of structure and restriction. All restrictions are more palatable if accompanied by explanations.

Fall clean-up days are really important. They can be times when gardeners dispose of diseased plants and when stakes, fencing, and other debris are taken up in preparation for fall plowing. One coordinator doesn't believe in fall plowing because organic matter that is plowed under won't rot in the wintertime and is just plowed up again in the spring. Needless to say, he has trouble getting gardeners to turn out for post-harvest clean-ups. There are other coordinators who believe that fall plowing exposes pests to winter conditions which considerably deplete their numbers next season. Gardeners who accept this turn out readily for fall clean-up.

One coordinator has a good solution to apathy about clean-up days; he states in his guidelines that a $10 fall clean-up deposit is required, along with the garden plot fee. The gardeners who show for clean-up get their deposit back; those who don't show have paid for the subsequent hiring of a clean-up crew. It works just the way an apartment deposit does and people don't seem to resent it as long as there is an adequate explanation given in the guidelines.

After these guidelines and restrictions have been established and written up as part of the enrollment form, it is time to advertise by distributing the forms to schools, housing projects, apartment complexes, YMCA's and YWCA's, or by an-nouncing the project through the newspaper or local radio stations. One co-ordinator started his project out by a single ad in the local paper. He got enough volunteer help in addition to plotters to prepare the site on a shoestring, and has had a 75-family project going ever since just by word of mouth over succeeding years. So all it took was the initial ad. Schoolchildren around the garden site can always be sent home with flyers or enrollment forms to show their parents if an all-out advertising campaign is needed or if the project is aiming to serve a large population. Posters can be put in supermarkets to remind shoppers that there is an alternative to outrageous prices. Good publicity helps in obtaining ongoing donations and funding, but much of this can be done more effectively by formal events held during the gardening season such as classes, workshops, and harvest festivities that involve the outer community.

After receipt of enrollment forms, the coordinator must assign plots and determine how many will be participating. Then confirmations and garden agreements must be sent to those who are assured of a plot. The agreement includes conditions and restrictions of the project, as well as rights to access, quiet, privacy, and so forth. Below is a sample garden agreement.[1] The plotter must sign and date the agreement.

SAMPLE

GARDENING AGREEMENT

Plot #_____

1. The premises shall be used solely as a personal garden in compliance with all rules and regulations of the City Beautiful Council relating to the community gardens project, as they may from time to time be amended.

2. The premises shall be maintained by participant in a clean, neat manner. Participant shall not cause damage or waste to the premises and shall not do or bring onto the premises anything which will in any way conflict with any law, ordinance, rule, or regulation; or use the property for any immoral or unlawful or improper purpose; or use the premises in any manner which will damage or annoy others.

3. Participant shall have the right of ingress to and from his(her) garden plot.

4. In the event waste is caused to or unnecessary damage be done to the premises by participant of any part or condition of this license or the rules and regulations be breached, the city may terminate this license and re-enter and repossess the plot, and this license shall cease. In the event of the above, participant may enter and harvest such crops as he has planted within 5 days after mailing such notice of default and termination. Such notice shall be deemed sufficient if sent regular mail postage prepaid to the licensee.

5. Participant may enter the premises for the purpose of establishing and maintaining garden on or about April 15, 1975, and shall harvest all crops no later than November 1, 1975, when this license shall end.

1. Drake, Susan York, *Recreational Community Gardening,* Bureau of Outdoor Recreation's Guide to Organization and Development, 1976, p. 21.

6. At termination of this license, participant shall return the premises to the city in a neat and orderly condition.

7. During the term of this agreement participant shall have the right to quiet enjoyment of the plot.

License granted by the City of Dayton, City Beautiful Council, this_____day of_____ 19____, to _____.

(Licensee)

The confirmation or garden agreement can include the plot number assignment and notice of a planning meeting. This planning meeting is sometimes combined with a spring workday on the site to prepare the plots for plowing. The planning meeting can introduce the coordinator, elect a site committee to oversee the plotters and enforce the guidelines, present soil analysis results, discuss apportionment and location of water, establish or present the policy on abandoned gardens, and establish tool-sharing procedures if tools are provided on the site. If tools are not provided, the following list can be passed out.

A PLOTTER'S LIST OF TOOLS

Hay fork
Pitchfork
Pointed Spade
Strong garden rake
Leaf Rake—bamboo or steel
Hoe
Hose
Watering can—one large and one medium
Trowel
Hand soil fork
Garden cart (the big one from Garden Way is best)
Paper cups or tin cans with ends out for cut-worm guards
Chicken wire for circular cylinders for tomatoes or squash
Stakes
Edger
Small hatchet for sharpening stakes at soil ends
Cold frame (optional)
Wire to run between stakes to support beans and peas

APPLICATION
LEBANON COMMUNITY GARDEN PROJECT

NAME: _____

ADDR: _____

TOWN: _____ CHOICE OF GARDEN SITE: _____

PHONE:_____ LOT   NUMBER   _____

Do you wish to obtain seeds and plants thru LISTEN? yes____ no____

                                                       Can not afford to pay.

Will you need canning supplies at end of garden season? yes____ no____

    Jars? qt. pt. ½ gal.   Lids? regular   wide-mouth

Total number of people benefitting from your garden plot? _____

I will help with the following committee: —*Public relations*/education (posters,

                                          news releases, etc.)

                                    —*Purchasing* (seeds, plants, tools)

                                    —*Physical needs* (plowing, staking-out plots,

                                    fertilizer).

Has the membership fee been paid? ($5.00 for 1 year/$1.25 for 3 months).

If no, when will it be paid? _____

RESPONSIBILITIES OF GARDENERS:

Each gardener shall:

(1) keep up their plot throughout the summer.

(2) place a small sign with your name in the front center of your lot.

(3) sign out each tool when borrowed and return them the same day.

(4) enter another's plot only when given prior permission.

(5) provide supervision when children and pets are with you in the garden.

(6) prevent your plants from wandering outside of your plot.

(7) keep alcoholic beverages away from the community garden site.

(8) be responsible for cleaning up your garden in the Fall.

(9) notify your fellow gardeners when they are violating the above rules.

     Each gardener is asked to actively participate in the work of garden committees. Repeated violation of the rules will mean forfeiture of your plot. These rules were drawn up (and agreed upon) for *your* protection.

     I have read the above list of "Responsibilities of Gardeners" and agree to abide by them.

                  /s/ _____

The Lebanon Community Garden Project is sponsored by: LISTEN

                                               60 Hanover St.

                                               Lebanon, N.H. 448-4553

GUIDELINES FOR THE COMMUNITY GARDEN
PROGRAM (H.O.M.E.)

1. Purpose - to make arable land available to those individuals who are eager to grow their own food (vegetables) and who do not have arable land to meet their needs. Priority will be given to those with greatest needs.

2. Two and one-half acres are available on the premises of H.O.M.E. Inc. to the Westerly side of the Education Building for this purpose.

3. Lots will be divided according to family size as best as we can determine.

4. A small fee of $5.00 for expenses will be charged for each lot and will be paid before the use of the lot.

5. It will be required to mark each garden plot with a number to distinguish garden plots.

6. The 2½ acres have been manured with aged chicken dressing and will be limed and roto-tilled. The soil test results show that the area can easily support vegetables.

7. Because of our purposes being organically oriented and to protect organic community gardeners, we urge all community gardeners to refrain from using dangerous chemicals, pesticides, and herbicides. Mild forms of chemical fertilizer are O.K.

8. Because of the serious dangers of weeds and weed seeds infesting our community garden and other neighboring farms we ask each plot be reasonably weed free. (Mustard, lambs quarters, perslane are some of the worst). One mustard plant gone to seed can infest a garden area to the point of dis-use for several years).

9. At the end of H.O.M.E.'s Craft Fair - Aug. 21st - a cash prize of $15.00 will be given to the best garden. A panel of judges will make periodic inspections of the garden plots during the season.

10. We would like a volunteer to be caretaker of the plots offering assistance and advice to other community gardeners if needed.

11. Please fill-in and return the attached form as soon as possible.

Send to: Down H.O.M.E. Farming - Community Garden Program
H.O.M.E. Co-op
Orland, Maine 04472

(H.O.M.E. application form continued)

Please note: All Questions need not be filled out. Excess lots will be given out as available.

ALL INFORMATION STRICTLY CONFIDENTIAL

Name_____Address_____Tel _____

Size of Family: No. of Adults_____No. of Children _____

Estimated Yearly Income _____

Source of Income_____

Do you receive Food Stamps? ( )yes ( )no

Are you interested in being the volunteer Community Garden Caretaker as stated in No. 10? ( )yes ( )no

Remarks: _____

Signed_____Date _____

- -

This is also the time to encourage Organics; examples of plot plans can be circulated that emphasize companion planting. Plotters should be advised to formulate a final plot plan which they keep and revise from year to year so that they can rotate crops if they like. There can also be a count of who would attend gardening classes, if available, and sign-up sheets can be circulated.

At the planning meeting there could be a talk by the coordinator or a visiting expert on land management, emphasizing what the community garden could be at its best. Systems for replenishing the soil resources could be discussed; composting could be presented, with simple recipes for constructing group piles along the edges of the plots. The spring workday could even include making compost boxes. Intensive gardening techniques could be discussed for maxiumum use of limited space. Raised beds could be constructed at spring workday in keeping with intensive methods.

The most essential spirit for the coordinator to impart at the initial planning meeting is one of enthusiasm and reverence for natural processes. This is usually contagious among beginning plotters, and can unite the project. Seed sources should also be discussed, especially with a view to succeeding years' savings in volume orders or keeping one's own seed. Canning supplies can also be pooled or sources shared to save money. The conditions of the past winter can be presented in an

LOS ANGELES NEIGHBORHOOD GARDENS AND FARMS

COMMUNITY GARDEN APPLICATION

NOTICE: This community garden is a potential primary source of food for you and
your family. As such, it deserves its due share of our full attention,
time and effort.

PLEASE FILL OUT ONLY ONE FORM FOR EACH INDIVIDUAL FAMILY OR GROUP:

NAME_____ HOME PHONE_____ WORK PHONE_____

ADDRESS_____ ZIP_____ DATE_____

NUMBER JOINING GARDEN_____ NAME_____ AGE_____

Gardeners may choose to participate in a communal plot and/or have an individual plot.
Check below to show your choice:

_____ INDIVIDUAL PLOT_____ COMMUNAL PLOT_____ BOTH

Each gardener in the communal plots may be required to devote about six hours a month,
perhaps more until it is fully planted. Gardening knowledge will be shared and
learned together. Please check below to show your availability.

TOTAL GARDENER HOUR
_____ 6 HOURS OK_____ MORE HOURS OK_____ WHOLE GROUP IS AVAILABLE

Besides the actual food-growing effort, there are other tasks that need volunteers to
make for a successful garden. The following committees are suggestions. Additions or
combinations of committee work may be made. Check below all your preferences.

_____SEED COMMITTEE: To poll all gardeners to find out what people want to plant;
to research best type of seed for that crop in this area; and how to plant
and care for it.

_____WATER COMMITTEE: To determine most efficient irrigation system; its cost,
installation requirements and maintenance; set watering schedules.

101

_____FERTILIZER COMMITTEE: To determine fertilizer needs, quantities and delivery schedules; construction of compost bins and piles.

_____NUTRITION COMMITTEE: To research nutritional elements of each vegetable; how to prepare it for eating, drying, canning and freezing.

_____COMMUNICATIONS COMMITTEE: To maintain a "phone squad" to keep all members up to date on garden activities; public relations to outside world; record garden history and regular newsletter; printing, copying and distribution of information; establish reference library.

_____COORDINATING COMMITTEE: Consists of all above committee chairpersons, overall chairperson, secretary and treasurer; sets dues; coordinates garden work schedules.

Please write below the vegetables you would like to grow, and check space if in a communal or individual plot.

VEGETABLE	COMMUNAL	INDIVIDUAL

Los Angeles Neighborhood Gardens and Farms is a joint effort of the Office of the Mayor of the City of Los Angeles and Metropolitan Neighborhood Gardens and Farms, Inc., a non-profit charitable organization.

Return to: Los Angeles Neighborhood Gardens and Farms
          Mayor Tom Bradley
          c/o

effort to predict the coming summer's rise in vegetable and fruit prices and the gardener's consequent savings.

The unity and enthusiasm generated at this initial planning meeting ought to give the coordinator extra confidence to go out and solicit donations of materials, funds, or services from local businesses and organizations. It is not uncommon for coordinators to find a contractor who will truck in free topsoil to a city garden, or to find generous city public works departments who will relocate a hydrant, or a forestry department to deliver a truckload of leaves or woodchips. One coordinator who gets truckloads of leaves from the town or private contractors year after year is trying to persuade his town to compost the sludge, which is sewage mixed with municipal trash, with leaves to use right on the gardens for fertilizer, rather than pouring it into the waterways. He is trying to convince the town officials that the phosphates in sludge should be recycled because our mineral supply is threatened and there are no substitutes for phosphates.

This same coordinator gets the use of the town's machines and services to plow and fertilize the site each year. Another coordinator of a large citywide project got Burpee's and Germain's, both national seed companies, to donate seed to the program. He got the Department of Public Works to disc the land and dig the trench to lay pipe to irrigate the plots. The $400 worth of pipe was bought with a Federal mini-grant.

CHAPTER 13

Preparing and Maintaining the Site

This successful solicitation of services, funds, and materials is essential to the next large step in organization: site preparation and maintenance. Plowing and discing the plots comes first; some gardening experts claim that plowing or rototilling the plot will massacre the earth worms. One such believer advises beginning gardeners to turn over the soil according to the trenching method.[1] Several coordinators claim, however, that their plots have the most earthworms per square foot of any garden in town and that they faithfully rototill every spring. While a few rare ones will trench, most beginning gardeners won't stay around that long since it is painstaking work and takes nearly all day for a 25 by 30 foot plot. Fortunately, most sites I visited have the use of machinery to prepare the soil, so the gardeners get to throw their energies into the more appealing jobs of arranging the space and planting. After the plowing, walkways, aisles, and recreation areas should be arranged. Trash cans, portable toilets, and bulletin boards should be installed. One garden site had the problem of vandals driving off at night with the trash cans. The coordinator chained them down and they were still taken, the chain just proving an extra challenge. This is rare though; vandalism is mainly limited to the pilfering of produce and no one really has a solution to this problem.

After walkways have been laid out, the plots can be staked out and identified, either by name or number, then located and posted on a map. It is a good idea to include space in this plan for a demonstration garden, as it provides the most tangible evidence of the benefits of any particular gardening methods the coordinator or garden staff is committed to. Recreation facilities, picnic tables, and tool-storage shelter should be provided where possible. If there is room, a volleyball court doesn't take much accompanying paraphernalia, and really adds alot to the garden experience. The net and ball can always be stored in the tool shed at night. A sandbox is not difficult to provide; it can be constructed out of lumber scraps, and it is the perfect imitation medium for toddlers who can't dig in the family plot. Nearly every site I visited had at least one picnic table. This seems to be the bare minimum for even the simplest sites, to provide a social focal point. A lot of coordinators eliminate the tool-storage and care problem by asking the

1. Smith, *Gardening For Food* (New York, Scribners, 1972) p. 10.

gardeners to bring their own. This is okay for the first few years, but having to keep a common set of tools intact and clean adds unity by adding one more shared responsibility.

Arrangements for water sources must be made. They can range from strategic positioning of rain barrels, through irrigation ditches and hoses, to pipes. In areas of the country where the water supply is threatened, irrigation systems are too costly to install and maintain; gardeners are encouraged to bring their own buckets, watering cans, and hoses, and a local resident is paid for the use of his water.

Arranging for the post-harvest site clean-up, autumn plowing, and planting of cover crops should be the last step in a site maintenance plan. If coordinators want to institute a deposit fee for clean-up day as previously mentioned, they can discuss this during the initial planning meeting as an idea for next year, or at succeeding meetings throughout the season. People should be informed of it in one of the guidelines or conditions published in the enrollment forms. Many coordinators, site committees, or garden committees have gotten stuck doing most of the clean-up, so it is essential that a clear and strict policy be formulated and implemented.

CHAPTER 14

Encouraging Communication

Encouraging communication is the final major step in organization. The pre-season garden meeting mentioned above is essential to establishing systems for continued contact throughout the season and, perhaps, the entire year. This meeting can determine gardeners' enthusiasm for such ideas as gardening classes, lectures by horticultural experts, and a monthly newsletter. As mentioned earlier, this is the time to encourage participation in a pre-season class on organic gardening if co-ordinators want to cut down on chemical gardeners. Some coordinators schedule picnics throughout the season so that gardeners may discuss insect and disease problems, vandalism, progress of growth, new gardening trends, and so forth.

One garden project continually imports speakers on such subjects as preserving techniques, freezing, canning, and solar drying, economy of space and motion in the garden, biodynamic composting, growth of community gardens across the country, establishment of cooperative canneries, gardening in the school systems, and construction of solar herb dryers or collectors to provide hot water to the tool-shed or restrooms. These lectures initiate a wide range of discussion and encourage innovation among the gardeners.

A bulletin board in a central location can be a colorful source of communication with displays on nutrition, the latest news releases about community gardens, gardening techniques, current vegetable prices for supermarket produce, and other items of interest. Along with these displays can be an envelope with recipes in it marked "Recipe Exchange." Each time a gardener finds a recipe he or she wants to try, he can take it, replacing it with another. This encourages people to start experimenting with combinations they don't often find in supermarkets, such as pumpkin and carrot breads, zucchini pickles and relishes, and corn pudding. There can also be an envelope where gardeners can drop routine questions or suggestions for the coordinator.

A monthly newsletter is one of the best ways to maintain communication and to assure a more stable population of applicants from season to season. In it each coming issue's deadline is given so that gardeners can contribute ideas. In many cases the coordinator ends up writing most of the newsletter, but one or two outside submissions are all that are needed to round out five or six pages, and that length will do the basic job of keeping gardeners in touch with their source. It can always include the application form for enrollment in the garden program plus the list of restrictions and regulations. The liveliest newsletters, despite their brevity, have cartoons, line drawings, and catchy titles like "Weed 'em and Reap."[1]

Arranging for gardeners to appear before community groups or on local talk shows is an effective means of advertising and education for the outer community. One program was televised as part of a series on land use throughout the state. The coordinator did not have to go searching for this publicity—the TV station approached her. Local garden clubs are curious about community gardening and are usually glad to have a gardener come and explain plotting to them. There are always conservation groups like the Audubon Society who welcome news from new grassroots ecological movements.

A distribution system for excess produce can spark community interest in a garden project. Donating the surplus to nursing homes or low-income housing projects assures publicity and community acceptance. A farm stand is another way to stimulate communication with the outer community; this could be set up just to distribute excess produce or to make a profit, although in the latter case, a farm stand should do more than $10,000 a year to profit. Some farm stands combine their local produce with items such as nuts and dried fruits from a food co-op organized side by side with the garden project. This provides the stand with a bigger variety, and produce can still be sold at competitive prices.

Another effective and necessary communication device is the evaluation of the season, usually solicited around harvest time by the coordinator. This way gardeners get to articulate their satisfactions and complaints, and sort of sum up the value of the program to themselves and to the coordinator. The coordinator gets feedback necessary for the report submitted to the sponsors of the program after harvest time. Contents of the report should include the number of families served, the total cost of the program and how much of this was offset by plot fees, the estimated savings per family from the plot yield, the current status of the lease, the need for more space and ideas for site expansion, the overall feeling about the program on the part of the gardeners, and their suggestions for improvements.

A harvest festival is a great celebrator of unity and provides a remembrance to stimulate future communication among gardeners and the outer community. This is often a public celebration, giving gardeners a chance to show off their produce or sell it to observers. There are often simple games for the kids like potato races and other field events, along with a harvest picnic of garden produce. Those projects with a barn can have hay-jumping and a barn-dance. These festivals are usually beautiful displays of unity and cooperation, with spirits running high and

1. Newsletter of Michigan State University Cooperative Extension Service, reproduced in Bureau of Outdoor Recreation's Guide To Recreational Community Gardening, op. cit. p. 65.

food weighing down the tables. They also provide some kind of needed resolution of the season, a tangible proof of the effort that gardeners put in. Every project, no matter how small, needs some such resolution or memories will gradually dim to neutrality during the winter months.

Communal Gardens

CHAPTER 15

The points of organization of a communal garden, that is to say, a one-plot garden in which everyone shares work and produce, would differ from the steps described for community gardens only in a few respects. The fee structure would be different, probably less per person or family because they would not be getting the privilege of planning and planting their own private plot. The development of a land-use program would be a bit different in terms of physical arrangement and land management. There would be more possibility of long-term pest control through crop rotation and companion planting, because with a single-plot garden, single species of vegetables are planted together—potatoes in a few rows here, corn in a patch at the north end, tomatoes in a special section, cold-weather and successive plantings in another section. A plan can be kept from year to year to assure crop rotation without much trouble. With a single plot there is a greater possibility of control, but to achieve it requires more work from the administration or the coordinator.

Planning the amount of space to provide each family with a season's worth of produce plus some to put up for the winter requires more sophisticated calculations than the simple assigning of a 25 by 30 foot plot as in the individual plot plan. The appendix has a table to plan how many row-feet will accommodate each person. Intensive or "postage-stamp" methods would require less space.[1] The successful communal gardens, such as the Ecology Center's Organic Garden in Ann Arbor, Michigan, have planned the size to suit a certain number of people, and then they limit their applicants to that number each year. They have also added space for what they term "small group gardens," which are individual plots for families or other units. The Ecology Center's application form and regulations have been included in the text as an example. Compared to the individual or community plots, the rules seem more strict and the responsibilities of the gardeners more clearly delineated. But it has been the prevalent experience of communal efforts that they fail because only a few members perform all the tasks while the rest of the gardeners tend to shirk their responsibilities. Thus, strict guidelines must be set up. On an individual plot site, it is perfectly clear who is working and who isn't,

1. Duane Newcomb, *The Postage Stamp Garden Book* (Los Angeles, J.P. Tarcher & Co., 1975).

and the consequences of sluffing off accrue mainly to the lazy ones—but on a communal site, every gardener must bear the brunt of any irresponsibility. The only way to avoid this is to establish the minimum working time that each individual must put in to be effective.

Because of the increased administrative control, the entire plot can be designated as organic only. One method can be used, such as French Intensive, trenching, or biodynamic planting; there is no room for mixtures as on individual-plot sites—the entire garden must be either organic or chemical. The most efficient way of designing a plot plan is for the coordinator to make a preliminary plan with a chart of the kinds and locations of all the basic vegetables according to principles of long-range pest control such as companion planting or rotation plans. Then at the preliminary pre-season garden meeting for all enrollees gardeners can examine the plan and make elaborations or adjustments according to their individual tastes in vegetables or flowers. If the entire plan were left wholly to the gardeners, there would probably be prolonged discussion over every proposed row. In something as complex as a garden plan that utilizes companion or rotation principles, one head is better than many. The finished plot plan should be posted on the bulletin board or in some central location at the site.

Just as there is a policy in a community garden for reclaiming of neglected or abandoned plots, there should be a policy (not delineated in the following example enrollment form) for those gardeners who do not put in their minimum working hours per week. It is hard to kick people out of an activity that is essentially set up for pleasure or recreation, but perhaps a talk with these people by the coordinator or garden committee is all that would be necessary. It is essential to discourage this lack of responsibility because it lowers the morale and makes a bad example, and those projects that were soft on such laziness have failed.

The sample enrollment form below includes the option of individual plots, (small group gardens):

Ecology Center's Organic Garden - 1976

Gardener's Responsibilities

1. Never use a pesticide, herbicide, or chemical fertilizer at the Organic Garden. Anyone doing so will be asked to leave.

2. Pest control on plots is a necessity. If you have a pest, find out how to control it. If plots are not cared for, within two weeks of a pest infestation, the garden will be rototilled. Other gardeners' vegetables should not be threatened by a few individuals' lack of care. This two week guideline applies to all vegetable growing areas.

3. Each gardener is expected to spend a minimum of three hours per week in addition

to the time spent harvesting: at least two hours per week working on the vegetable plots and at least one hour per week on general maintenance tasks for the garden.

4. Each gardener is expected to help with the preparation and be at the garden June 12th for the Rite of Spring.

5. Fall clean-up is an essential part of summer gardening and ALL gardeners should expect to help in this effort. Small group gardeners whose plots are not cleared in the fall will not be allowed to garden the following year.

6. All gardeners should take care of the tools by cleaning them as needed and making sure that they are put away when done. Also, minor repairs should be done as needed or we are apt to end up with a tool shed full of broken tools. If the repair job is extensive or beyond your time and/or knowledge, please let a member of the coordinating committee know.

7. Inexperienced gardeners should plan to attend the orientation sessions (including principles of organic gardening, tour, use of tools, etc.) to be scheduled in early spring. We think you will find them quite helpful.

8. If you have questions regarding gardening, pests, harvesting, etc., as you are gardening, refer to the references in the shed. If still in doubt, be sure to ask!

1976 Organic Garden Participation Form

I agree with and understand the gardener's responsibilities.

NAME(S) _____

_____

ADDRESS _____ CITY AND ZIP _____

PHONE NOS.: HOME _____ WORK _____

Garden participation desired:

1. Community Gardener _____ How much previous organic
2. Small Group Gardener _____ gardening experience do
   Names of other group members: you have?_____years.

As part of each gardener's general maintenance duties, routine tasks must be done and special problems tackled. Please check (✓) below five interests you would be willing to work on during the gardening season.

____flowers ____fallow and green manure
____erosion ____tools (do you have skill
____varmint control in small engine re-
____mulch and manure pairs?)
  yes____ no____

ORGANIZING A COMMUNITY GARDEN

____compost

____collective herb garden

____carpentry

____tree care

____fruits (berries, grapes)

____signs and labels

____education

____organic research

____publicity

____Rite of Spring coordination

Please list below any possible material resources or skills you possess or have access to (i.e. truck, stakes, twine, repair skills, etc.):

Appendix

A MONTHLY CHECKLIST OF ACTIVITIES AND TASKS[1]

The following monthly checklist of activities and tasks summarizes the basic steps necessary for a successful recreational community gardening program. This checklist assumes that the last frost would occur May 1. To adjust to weather in different zones, refer to the map and equate the month of your last frost with the end of April or first of May.

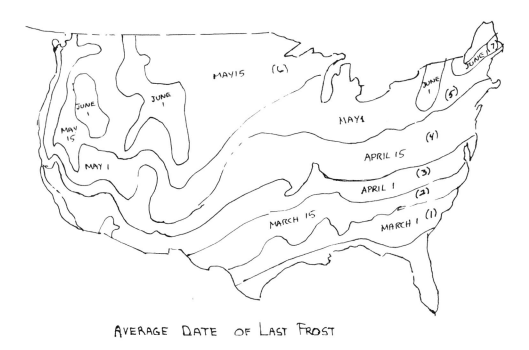

AVERAGE DATE OF LAST FROST

---

1. From Bureau of Outdoor Recreation Booklet: *Recreational Community Gardening*, pp. 40-43.

Monthly Checklist

Month	Activities and Tasks	Comments
Preseason		
January	Prepare budget detailing financial need for all aspects of gardening project and its associated recreation programs.	
	Identify and approach sources of financial assistance, both public and private; determine fee structure.	
	Plan and implement fund raising activities and strategies.	
	Obtain assistance of horticultural expert; develop land use management program.	
	Select site and obtain formal land use commitment.	
	Establish goals and objectives of the education programs, gardening skills, canning, nutrition, etc.	
	Assess the community resources and opportunities which may contribute to the education programs.	
February	Recruit paid or volunteer coordinators.	
	Obtain insurance.	
	Develop site plan.	
	Develop guidelines.	
	Advertise the availability of land and programs	

through posters, TV, radio, newspapers, personal visits.

Prepare enrollment form and distribute to schools, gardeners, housing projects, recreation department, cooperative extension service, neighborhood centers, libraries, etc.

Arrange for plowing and site preparation.

Locate and procure equipment, materials, and labor for site development.

March   Train volunteer or paid site coordinators and assistants.

Confirm plowing and site preparation arrangements.

Solicit donations of materials and services.

Encourage participation and advertise the need for land, funds, materials, and labor.

Record data and assign people to plots upon receipt of enrollment forms.

Coordinate the development and installation of recreation facilities, creative playgrounds, rest areas.

Close enrollment.

Arrange for water sources, including rain barrels,

Month	Activities and Tasks	Comments
	hoses, buckets, irrigation ditches, and pipes.	
	Assess need for tools, purchase as required, and provide for tool sharing procedures.	
Garden Season		
April	Plow and disc sites.	
	Stake out individual plots.	
	Begin educational programs with a preseason garden class.	
	Begin gardening if weather permits.	
	Hold preseason meeting with gardeners.	
May	Establish garden committee.	
June		
July		
August	Develop and maintain demonstration garden.	
	Serve as catalyst for organized recreational activities such as formation of volleyball teams, scheduled picnics, outdoor movies (if electricity available).	
	Conduct garden class on insect and disease problems.	
	Hold demonstrations on canning and freezing techniques.	
	Collect and exchange recipes.	

Month	Activities and Tasks	Comments	APPENDIX
	Assist gardeners and outside groups with requests for special activities, tours, parties.		
	Prepare news releases on a continuing basis.		
	Arrange for gardeners to appear on local talk shows and before community groups.		
	Write monthly newsletter.		
	Set up distribution system for surplus produce.		
Harvest and Wrap-up			
September	Conduct evaluation survey of gardeners.		
	Continue harvest.		
	Begin fund raising for next season.		
	Host harvest festival.		
October	Evaluate yield.		
November	Continue harvest.		
	Plow and plant green manure/cover crops.		
	Continue fund raising.		
	Repair and store tools and equipment for winter.		
	Write site coordinator report.		

SAMPLE PLOT LAYOUT FOR WARM REGIONS
California and the Gulf of Mexico with
Last Frost Between January 30 and March 10
(Including Zones 1 and 2 of map on page 113)
Principles of Companion Planting Observed
←— *25 Feet* —→

N
↑
↓
S

36 inches	Irish Potatoes (January) followed by Corn (March)
24 inches	Cabbage—divide row in thirds and plant in (January) successive weeks for continuous harvest
18 inches	Onions—successively cropped (January)
18 inches	Turnips (January) followed by Peppers (April)
12 inches	Radishes intercropped with Garlic (January)
18 inches	Sea Kale (January) followed by Endive (March)
24 inches	Collards (January) followed by Soybeans (March)
24 inches	Lettuce—successively cropped (February)
36 inches	Tomatoes (March)
18 inches	Mustard—successively cropped (February)
24 inches	Peanuts (March)
18 inches	Peas (January) followed by Cress (February)
48 inches	Cantaloupes (March)
48 inches	Watermelon or Squash (April) (March)

←— 30 Feet —→

SAMPLE PLOT LAYOUT FOR MODERATE REGIONS
Pennsylvania through Middle West to Oregon and Washington
Last Frost between March 20 and May 10
(Zones 3 and 4 of map on page 113)

N
↑
↓
S

Principles of Companion Planting Observed

← 25 Feet →

36 inches	Peas (January) followed by Cauliflower (April)
24 inches	Spinach (February) followed by Bush Beans (April)
18 inches	Carrots — divide row into thirds and plant each section in successive weeks for continuous harvest (March)
18 inches	Swiss Chard (March)
12 inches	Onions intercropped with Leeks (March)
18 inches	Lettuce successively cropped (March)
24 inches	Brussels Sprouts successively cropped (March)
24 inches	Potatoes successively cropped (March)
36 inches	Tomatoes (April)
18 inches	Corn Salad (February)
24 inches	Cucumbers successively cropped (May)
18 inches	Peppers successively cropped (April)
48 inches	Cantaloupe (April)
48 inches	Watermelon or Squash (April)

↑
30 Feet
↓

119

SAMPLE PLOT LAYOUT FOR COLD REGIONS
Upper Western States and New England
Last frost between May 10 and June 1
(Zones 5, 6 and 7 of map on page 113)

N
S

Principles of Companion Planting Observed

← 25 Feet →

36 inches	Corn successively cropped — divide row in thirds — plant each third in successive weeks (May)
24 inches	Carrots successively cropped (April)
18 inches	Beets successively cropped (April)
18 inches	Turnips successively cropped (April)
12 inches	Onions intercropped with Radishes (April)
18 inches	Swiss Chard successively cropped (May)
24 inches	Lettuce successively cropped (April)
24 inches	Cabbage successively cropped (April)
36 inches	Tomatoes (June)
18 inches	Bush Beans successively cropped (May)
24 inches	Spinach (April) followed by Cucumbers (May)
18 inches	Peas (February) followed by Peppers (May)
48 inches	Muskmelons (May)
48 inches	Summer Squash (May)

← 30 Feet →

PLANTING CHART[1]

Crop	Suggested feet of row or amount per person*****	Seeds or plants (P) required per 100 feet of row	Planting Distance (Inches) Between rows	Planting Distance (Inches) Between plants or Hills (H)	Depth of planting (Inches)	Time for seeding or transplanting in garden (Zone 5)*****
Asparagus	15-20	60-70 (P)	36-48	18	6-8	May 10-20 roots
Beans						
Pole	10	½ lb.	36	24 (H)	1	June 1-5
Snap	20-30*	¾ lb.	24	2-4	1	June 1-5
Beets	10-15*	1 oz.	12-18	2-3	½	May 1-15 June 20-Late crop
Broccoli**	5 plants	1/8 oz. or 67 (P)	24-30	18-20	¼	May 1 plants
Cabbage						
Early**	5 plants	1/8 oz. or 67-100 (P)	24-30	18	¼	May 1 plants June 20 plants
Late	10 plants					
Carrots	50-75	½ oz.	12-18	2-3	½	April 20-May 10 June 20-Late crop
Cauliflower**	5	1/8 oz. or 67 (P)	24-30	12-18	¼	May 10 plants
Swiss Chard	5	1 oz.	18-24	6-8	½	April 25-May 10
Sweet Corn						
Early	20	¼ lb.	24-36	6	1	May 20
Midseason	20			8		very early crop
Late	40			9		June 1-5 main crop
Cucumbers	10-15	½ oz.	48	48 (H)	¾	June 1

1. Adapted from Bulletin 544 of the Maine Cooperative Extension Service, *Home Vegetable Gardening*, by W.H. Erhardt, pp. 10-12.

    *   Make two or more plantings or plant early, midseason, and late varieties at same time. Suggested amount is for each planting.

   **   Depth of planting refers to seeding depth indoors.

  ***   Planting distance is for both types. If large vine types are planted allow more space.

 ****   If only early varieties are planted, allow 15 plants per person. If main crop varieties are grown, plant 8 to 10 plants per person.

*****   The exact date may vary with the season, soil type and local planting conditions. In southern Zone 5 the early plantings may be made 10 days to two weeks earlier and the late plantings 10 days to two weeks later.

******   Assuming you freeze, store and can vegetables at home, these are the vegetable needs per person.

Crop	Suggested feet of row or amount per person******	Seeds or plants (P) required per 100 feet of row	Planting Distance (Inches) Between rows	Planting (Inches) Between plants or hills (H)	Depth of planting (Inches)	Time for seeding or transplanting in garden (Zone 5)*****
Lettuce						
Head**	5-10*	¼ oz. or 75-100 (P)	12-18	15-18	¼	May 1-July 1
Leaf	5*	¼ oz.	12-18	6	¼	May 1-July 1
Melons**						
Muskmelons	10-25	½ oz. or 60-100 (P)	48	48 (H)	¾	June 1-5
Watermelons	10-15	1 oz. or 50-60 (P)	72	60 (H)	¾	June 1-5
Onions	10-20	1 lb. (sets) or ½ oz.	12-18	1-3	½	May 1-15 sets & seeds
Parsnips	5-10	½ oz.	18-24	2-4	½	May 1-15
Peas (Early & Late)	50-150*	1 lb.	18-36	1-2	1	April 20-25 (early) May 20-June 5 (late)
Peppers**	2 plants	1 pkt. or 67 (P)	18-24	18	¼	June 1-5
Pumpkins***	1 hill	1 oz.	36	48 (H)	1	June 1
Radishes	5*	1 oz.	12-18	1	½	April 20-June 10
Rhubarb	5-10	40-50 (P)	48	24-30	2-3	May 1 roots
Rutabagas	10-20	¼ oz.	18-24	6-8	½	June 15
Spinach	25*	1 oz.	12-18	3-4	½	April 25-May 10
Squash***						
Summer	1 hill	1 oz.	36	48 (H)	1	June 1
Winter	20-30	1 oz.	72-96	72 (H)	1	June 1
Tomatoes**	15 plants****	1 pkt. or 25-67 (P)	24-48	18-48	¼	June 1-5
Turnips	10-15	¼ oz.	15-18	3-5	½	April 25-May 10

    * Make two or more plantings or plant early, midseason, and late varieties at same time. Suggested amount is for each planting.

    ** Depth of planting refers to seeding depth indoors.

    *** Planting distance is for both types. If large vine types are planted allow more space.

    **** If only early varieties are planted, allow 15 plants per person. If main crop varieties are grown, plant 8 to 10 plants per person.

    ***** The exact date may vary with the season, soil type and local planting conditions. In southern Zone 5 the early plantings may be made 10 days to two weeks earlier and the late plantings 10 days to two weeks later.

    ****** Assuming you freeze, store and can vegetables at home, these are the vegetable needs per person.

Vegetable	Amount of seed	Space Needed (Feet of Row)	Estimated Production
Beans, Snap	2 oz.	15	7 lbs.
Beets	¼ oz.	25	25 lbs.
Broccoli	12 plants	25	10 lbs.
Brussels Sprouts	15 plants	25	8 lbs.
Cabbage	6 plants	12	6 heads
Carrots	½ pkt.	15	15 lbs.
Cauliflower	5 plants	10	5 heads
Celery	30 plants	15	30 stalks
Cucumbers	½ pkt.	10	6 lbs.
Eggplant	3 plants	6	12 fruits
Endive	10 plants	6	10 heads
Leeks	1 pkt.	10	30 plants
Lettuce (head)	18 plants	15	15 heads
Lettuce (leaf)	1 pkt.	5	2½ lbs.
Muskmelon	½ pkt.	16	18 fruits
Onion (sets)	½ lb.	10	5 lbs.
Onion (transplants)	120 each	30	25 lbs.
Onion (seeds)	1 pkt.	30	25 lbs.
Parsnips	1/3 pkt.	15	15 lbs.
Peas	1 lb.	100	28 lbs.
Peppers	6 plants	10	6 lbs.
Potatoes	5 lbs.	50	50 lbs.
Pumpkins	1/3 pkt.	3 hills	30 lbs.
Radishes	1 pkt.	12	8 lbs.
Spinach	1/8 oz.	10	5 lbs.
Squash (Summer)	½ pkt.	2 hills	24 fruits
Squash (Winter)	1 pkt.	4 hills	10 fruits
Sweet Corn	¼ lb.	25 (2 rows)	40 ears
Tomatoes	10 plants	40	3 bushels
Turnips	1/8 pkt.	20	20 lbs.

*Yields are for the extent of the growing season (zones 1 through 7). From Bureau of Outdoor Recreation Booklet, p. 63.

NUTRITIVE VALUES OF THE EDIBLE PART OF VEGETABLES AND VEGETABLE PRODUCTS[1]
(Dashes in the columns for nutrients show that no suitable value could be found
although there is reason to believe that a measurable amount of the nutrient may
be present.)

Vegetable, approximate measure, and weight (in grams)		Water (percent)	Food Energy (Cal.)	Protein (Grams)	Fat (Grams)	Carbo-hydrate (Grams)
Asparagus, green:	Grams					
Cooked, drained:						
Spears, ½ in. diam.						
at base 4 spears	60	94	10	1	Trace	2
Pieces, 1½ to 2 in.						
lengths 1 cup	145	94	30	3	Trace	5
Canned, solids and						
liquid 1 cup	244	94	45	5	1	7
Beans:						
Lima, immature 1 cup	170	71	190	13	1	34
seeds, cooked drained						
Snap:						
Green:						
Cooked, drained 1 cup	125	92	30	2	Trace	7
Canned, solids 1 cup	239	94	45	2	Trace	10
and liquid						
Yellow or wax:						
Cooked, drained 1 cup	125	93	30	2	Trace	6
Canned, solids 1 cup	239	94	45	2	1	10
and liquid						
Sprouted mung beans						
cooked, drained—1 cup	125	91	35	4	Trace	7
Beets:						
Cooked, drained, peeled:						
Whole beets, 2 in. diam.						
2 beets	100	91	30	1	Trace	7
Diced or sliced 1 cup	170	91	55	2	Trace	12
Canned, solids and						
liquid 1 cup	246	90	85	2	Trace	19
Beet greens, leaves and						
stems, cooked, drained						
1 cup	145	94	25	3	Trace	5
Blackeye peas (See						
Cowpeas)						

1. Adapted from U.S. Department of Agriculture Bulletin No. 72, pp. 13-18.

Calcium (Milligrams)	Iron (Milligrams)	Vitamin A value (International Units)	Thiamine (Milligrams)	Riboflavin (Milligrams)	Niacin (Milligrams)	Ascorbic acid (Milligrams)
13	.4	540	.10	.11	.8	16
30	.9	1,310	.23	.26	2.0	38
44	4.1	1,240	.15	.22	2.0	37
80	4.3	480	.31	.17	2.2	29
63	.8	680	.09	.11	.6	15
81	2.9	690	.07	.10	.7	10
63	0.8	290	.09	.11	.6	16
81	2.9	140	.07	.10	.7	12
21	1.1	30	.11	.13	.9	8
14	.5	20	.03	.04	.3	6
24	.9	30	.05	.07	.5	10
34	1.5	20	.02	.05	.2	7
144	2.8	7,400	.10	.22	.4	22

Vegetable, approximate measure, and weight (in grams)		Water (percent)	Food Energy (Cal.)	Protein (Grams)	Fat (Grams)	Carbo-hydrate (Grams)
Broccoli, cooked, drained:	Grams					
Whole stalks, medium size						
1 stalk	180	91	45	6	1	8
Stalks cut into ½ in.						
pieces—1 cup	155	91	40	5	1	7
Chopped, yield from						
10 oz. frozen pkg. 13/8 cups						
	250	92	65	7	1	12
Brussels sprouts, 7-8						
sprouts (1¼ to 1½ in.						
diam.) per cup, cooked						
1 cup	155	88	55	7	1	10
Cabbage:						
Common varieties:						
Raw:						
Coarsely shredded						
or sliced—1 cup	70	92	15	1	Trace	4
Finely shredded						
or chopped—1 cup	90	92	20	1	Trace	5
Cooked: 1 cup	145	94	30	2	Trace	6
Red, raw, coarsely						
shredded—1 cup	70	90	20	1	Trace	5
Savoy, raw, coarsely						
shredded—1 cup	70	92	15	2	Trace	3
Cabbage, celery or						
Chinese, raw, cut						
in 1 in. pieces—1 cup	75	95	10	1	Trace	2
Cabbage, spoon (or						
pakchoy), cooked—1 cup	170	95	25	2	Trace	4
Carrots:						
Raw:						
Whole, 5½ by 1 inch						
1 carrot (25 thin						
strips)	50	88	20	1	Trace	5
Grated 1 cup	110	88	45	1	Trace	11
Cooked, diced 1 cup	145	91	45	1	Trace	10
Canned, strained or						
chopped (baby food)						
1 oz.	28	92	10	Trace	Trace	2

Calcium (Milligrams)	Iron (Milligrams)	Vitamin A value (International Units)	Thiamine (Milligrams)	Riboflavin (Milligrams)	Niacin (Milligrams)	Ascorbic acid (Milligrams)
158	1.4	4,500	.16	.36	1.4	162
136	1.2	3,880	.14	.31	1.2	140
135	1.8	6,500	.15	.30	1.3	143
50	1.7	810	.12	.22	1.2	135
34	.3	90	.04	.04	.2	33
44	.4	120	.05	.05	.3	42
64	.4	190	.06	.06	.4	48
29	.6	30	.06	.04	.3	43
47	.6	140	.04	.06	.2	39
32	.5	110	.04	.03	.5	19
252	1.0	5,270	.07	.14	1.2	26
18	.4	5,500	.03	.03	.3	4
41	.8	12,100	.06	.06	.7	9
48	.9	15,220	.08	.07	.7	9
7	.1	3,690	.01	.01	.1	1

Vegetable, approximate measure, and weight (in grams)	Water (percent)	Food Energy (Cal.)	Protein (Grams)	Fat (Grams)	Carbo-hydrate (Grams)
Cauliflower, cooked, flowerbuds—1 cup	Grams 120	93	25	3	Trace	5
Celery, raw:					
Stalk, large outer, 8 by about 1½ inches, at root end 1 stalk	40	94	5	Trace	Trace	2
Pieces, diced—1 cup	100	94	15	1	Trace	4
Collards, cooked—1 cup	190	91	55	5	1	9
Corn, sweet:					
Cooked, ear 5 by 1 ear 1¾ in.²	140	74	70	3	1	16
Canned, solids and liquid—1 cup	256	81	170	5	2	40
Cowpeas, cooked, immature seeds—1 cup	160	72	175	13	1	29
Cucumbers, 10 oz.; 7½ by about 2 in.:					
Raw, pared 1 cucumber	207	96	30	1	Trace	7
Raw, pared, center slice, 1/8″ thick—6 slices	50	96	5	Trace	Trace	2
Dandelion greens, cooked 1 cup	180	90	60	4	1	12
Endive, curly (including Escarole) 2 oz.	57	93	10	1	Trace	2
Kale, leaves including stems, cooked 1 cup	110	91	30	4	1	4
Lettuce, raw:					
Butterhead, as Boston types; head, 4 in. diameter—1 head	220	95	30	3	Trace	6

2. Measure and weight apply to entire vegetable including parts not usually eaten.

3. Based on yellow varieties; white varieties contain only a trace of cryptoxanthin and carotenes, the pigments in corn that have biological activity.

Calcium (Milligrams)	Iron (Milligrams)	Vitamin A value (International Units)	Thiamine (Milligrams)	Riboflavin (Milligrams)	Niacin (Milligrams)	Ascorbic acid (Milligrams)
25	.8	70	.11	.10	.7	66
16	.1	100	.01	.01	.1	4
39	.3	240	.03	.03	.3	9
289	1.1	10,260	.27	.37	2.4	87
2	.5	310³	.09	.08	1.0	7
10	1.0	690³	.07	.12	2.3	13
38	3.4	560	.49	.18	2.3	28
35	.6	Trace	.07	.09	.4	23
8	.2	Trace	.02	.02	.1	6
252	3.2	21,060	.24	.29	—	32
46	1.0	1,870	.04	.08	.3	6
147	1.3	8,140	—	—	—	68
77	4.4	2,130	.14	.13	.6	18

Vegetable, approximate measure, and weight (in grams)		Water (percent)	Food Energy (Cal.)	Protein (Grams)	Fat (Grams)	Carbo-hydrate (Grams)
Lettuce, (cont.)	Grams					
Crisphead, as Iceberg; head 4¾ in. diam.						
1 head	454	96	60	4	Trace	13
Looseleaf, or bunching varieties, leaves						
2 large	50	94	10	1	Trace	2
Mushrooms, canned, solids and liquid						
1 cup	244	93	40	5	Trace	6
Mustard greens, cooked						
1 cup	140	93	35	3	1	6
Okra, cooked, pod						
3 by ¾ in.—8 pods	85	91	25	2	Trace	5
Onions:						
Mature:						
Raw, 2½ in. diam.						
1 onion	110	89	40	2	Trace	10
Cooked—1 cup	210	92	60	3	Trace	14
Young green, small, without tops—6 onions	50	88	20	1	Trace	5
Parsley, raw, chopped						
1 tbsp.	4	85	Trace	Trace	Trace	Trace
Parsnips, cooked—1 cup	155	82	100	2	1	23
Peas, green:						
Cooked—1 cup	160	82	115	9	1	19
Canned, solids and liquid—1 cup	249	83	165	9	1	31
Canned, strained (baby food) 1 oz.	28	86	15	1	Trace	3
Peppers, hot, red, without seeds, dried (ground chili powder, added seasonings)						
1 tbsp.	15	8	50	2	2	8
Peppers, sweet:						
Raw, about 5 per lb.:						
Green pod minus stem and seeds—1 pod	74	93	15	1	Trace	4

130

Calcium (Milligrams)	Iron (Milligrams)	Vitamin A value (International Units)	Thiamine (Milligrams)	Riboflavin (Milligrams)	Niacin (Milligrams)	Ascorbic acid (Milligrams)
91	2.3	1,500	.29	.27	1.3	29
34	.7	950	.03	.04	.2	9
15	1.2	Trace	.04	.60	4.8	4
193	2.5	8,120	.11	.19	.9	68
78	.4	420	.11	.15	.8	17
30	.6	40	.04	.04	.2	11
50	.8	80	.06	.06	.4	14
20	.3	Trace	.02	.02	.2	12
8	.2	340	Trace	.01	Trace	7
70	.9	50	.11	.12	.2	16
37	2.9	860	.44	.17	3.7	33
50	4.2	1,120	.23	.13	2.2	22
3	.4	140	.02	.02	.4	3
40	2.3	9,750	.03	.17	1.3	2
7	.5	310	.06	.06	.4	94

Vegetable, approximate measure, and weight (in grams)		Water (percent)	Food Energy (Cal.)	Protein (Grams)	Fat (Grams)	Carbo-hydrate (Grams)
Peppers, sweet, (cont.)	Grams					
Cooked, boiled, drained						
1 pod	73	95	15	1	Trace	3
Potatoes, medium (about 3 per pound raw):						
Baked, peeled after baking						
1 potato	99	75	90	3	Trace	21
Boiled:						
Peeled after boiling						
1 potato	136	80	105	3	Trace	23
Peeled before boiling						
1 potato	122	83	80	2	Trace	18
French-fried, piece 2 by ½ by ½ inch:						
Cooked in deep fat						
10 pieces	57	45	155	2	7	20
Frozen, heated						
10 pieces	57	53	125	2	5	19
Mashed:						
Milk added—1 cup	195	83	125	4	1	25
Milk and butter						
added: 1 cup	195	80	185	4	8	24
Potato Chips, medium,						
2 in. diam. 10 chips	20	2	115	1	8	10
Pumpkin, canned—1 cup	228	90	75	2	1	18
Radishes, raw, small,						
without tops—4 rad.	40	94	5	Trace	Trace	1
Sauerkraut, canned, solids						
and liquid—1 cup	235	93	45	2	Trace	9
Spinach:						
Cooked 1 cup	180	92	40	5	1	6
Canned, drained solids						
1 cup	180	91	45	5	1	6
Squash, Cooked:						
Summer, diced 1 cup	210	96	30	2	Trace	7
Winter, baked,						
mashed 1 cup	205	81	130	4	1	32

Calcium (Milligrams)	Iron (Milligrams)	Vitamin A value (International Units)	Thiamine (Milligrams)	Riboflavin (Milligrams)	Niacin (Milligrams)	Ascorbic acid (Milligrams)
7	.4	310	.05	.05	.4	70
9	.7	Trace	.10	.04	1.7	20
10	.8	Trace	.13	.05	2.0	22
7	.6	Trace	.11	.04	1.4	20
9	.7	Trace	.07	.04	1.8	12
5	1.0	Trace	.08	.01	1.5	12
47	.8	50	.16	.10	2.0	19
47	.8	330	.16	.10	1.9	18
8	.4	Trace	.04	.01	1.0	3
57	.9	14,590	.07	.12	1.3	12
12	.4	Trace	.01	.01	.1	10
85	1.2	120	.07	.09	.4	33
167	4.0	14,580	.13	.25	1.0	50
212	4.7	14,400	.03	.21	.6	24
52	.8	820	.10	.16	1.6	21
57	1.6	8,610	.10	.27	1.4	27

Vegetable, approximate measure, and weight (in grams)	Water (percent)	Food Energy (Cal.)	Protein (Grams)	Fat (Grams)	Carbo-hydrate (Grams)
Sweet potatoes: Grams					
Cooked, medium, 5 by 2 in., weight raw about 6 oz.:					
Baked, peeled after baking					
1 sweet potato	110	64	155	2	1	36
Boiled, peeled after boiling					
1 sweet potato	147	71	170	2	1	39
Candied, 3½ by 2¼ inches					
1 sweet potato	175	60	295	2	6	60
Canned, vacuum or					
solid pack—1 cup	218	72	235	4	Trace	54
Tomatoes:					
Raw, approx. 3 in. diam. 2 1/8 in. high;					
wt., 7 oz. 1 tomato	200	94	40	2	Trace	9
Canned, solids and					
liquid 1 cup	241	94	50	2	1	10
Tomato Catsup:					
Cup 1 cup	273	69	290	6	1	69
Tablespoon 1 tbsp.	15	69	15	Trace	Trace	4
Tomato juice, canned:					
Cup 1 cup	243	94	45	2	Trace	10
Glass (6 fl. oz.)					
1 glass	182	94	35	2	Trace	8
Turnips, cooked, diced					
1 cup	155	94	35	1	Trace	8
Turnip greens, cooked					
1 cup	145	94	30	3	Trace	5

4. Year round average. Samples marketed from November through May, average 20 milligrams per 200 gram tomato; from June through October, around 52 milligrams.

Calcium (Milligrams)	Iron (Milligrams)	Vitamin A value (Interna-tional Units)	Thiamine (Milligrams)	Riboflavin (Milligrams)	Niacin (Milligrams)	Ascorbic acid (Milligrams)
44	1.0	8,910	.10	.07	7	24
47	1.0	11,610	.13	.09	.9	25
65	1.6	11,030	.10	.08	.8	17
54	1.7	17,000	.10	.10	1.4	30
24	.9	1,640	.11	.07	1.3	42*
14	1.2	2,170	.12	.07	1.7	41
60	2.2	3,830	.25	.19	4.4	41
3	.1	210	.01	.01	.2	2
17	2.2	1,940	.12	.07	1.9	39
13	1.6	1,460	.09	.05	1.5	29
54	.6	Trace	.06	.08	.5	34
252	1.5	8,270	.15	.33	.7	68

NATURAL PEST CONTROL GUIDE[1]

	Control Agent:	Birds	Oil	Pyrethrum	Rotenone	Ryania	Sabadilla	Thuringiensis	Sulphur	Beneficial Insects
	Ants	X		X						X
	Aphids	X	X	X	X	X				X
	Mealybugs	X	X							X
	Scale	X	X							X
	Mites		X		X	X			X	X
	Caterpillars	X		X	X	X	X	X	X	X
	Moths	X				X		X		
Pests	Leafhoppers	X		X	X	X	X		X	X
	Borers					X				X
	Snails and Slugs	X								X
	Thrips		X	X	X	X				X
	Beetles and True Bugs	X		X	X	X	X		X	
	Powdery Mildew								X	
	Rust								X	
	Leaf Spot		X							

1. Cooperative Extension Service of Maine Bulletin 567, *Natural Gardening*, p. 18.

136

REPELLENT PLANTS AND PEST INFESTATIONS

Repellent Plant	Pest	Desired Plant
Asparagus	Soil Insects	Tomato
Bean	Colorado Potato Beetle	Potato
Chive	Scab	Apple
Celery	White Cabbage Butterfly	Cole Crops
Flax	Colorado Potato Beetle	Potato
Hemp	Cabbage Maggot	Cole Crops
Herbs	Cabbage Maggot	Cole Crops
	Carrot Fly	Carrot
	Flea Beetle	Radish
Leek	Carrot Fly	Carrot
Lettuce (Head)	Flea Beetle	Radish
Marigold (African & French)	Nematodes	Potato, Rose & Tomato
Mint	Ant	— — —
	Cabbage Maggot	Cole Crops
	White Cabbage Butterfly	Cole Crops
Mole Plant	Moles and Mice	Trees
Nasturtium	Aphid	Apple, Cole Crops & Radish
	Squash Bug	Vine Crops
	White Fly	Greenhouse Crops
Onion	Carrot Fly	Carrot
Radish	Cucumber Beetle	Vine Crops
Tomato	Asparagus Beetle	Asparagus
	Cabbage Maggot	Cole Crops
	White Cabbage Butterfly	Cole Crops

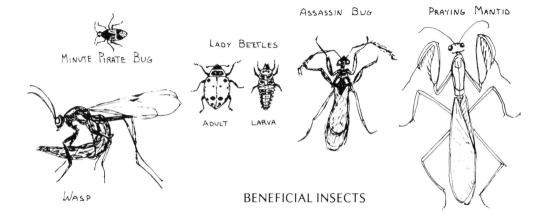

MINUTE PIRATE BUG

LADY BEETLES

ADULT   LARVA

ASSASSIN BUG

PRAYING MANTID

WASP

BENEFICIAL INSECTS

pH SCALE (SOIL REACTIONS)*

Soil Reaction	pH	Plant Requirements
	10.0	
Strongly Alkaline	9.0	
Medium Alkaline	8.0	
Slightly Alkaline	7.5	
Neutral	7.0	The great majority of home-ground plants thrive best within this pH range.
Slightly Acid	6.5	
Medium Acid	6.0	
	5.5	Azalea, Laurel, Pieris, Blueberry, Watermelon, Potato, and Rhododendron grow best within this range.
Strongly Acid	5.0	
	4.5	
Very Strongly Acid	4.0	
	3.5	

*From Bulletin 567 of Cooperative Extension Service of University of Maine, *Natural Gardening*, p. 14.

General

Your neighbor—a walk through your neighborhood will tell you who to seek out for advice on what to plant where and when, because a person who is familiar with growing in conditions unique to his own area is the best gardening friend to cultivate. Such a friend will also be attuned to the latest community efforts to organize plot sites, or might be a potential organizer himself.

The local extension service horticultural expert is a goldmine of information, and will presumably be informed of any community efforts being initiated. Offices are in nearly every county in the U.S. and are listed in the phone book under the county government.

Local Garden clubs.

Garden supply dealers.

Local nurserymen.

Radio and TV garden programs.

Publications of the Agricultural Research Service, Cooperative State Research Service, Forest Service, and Soil Conservation Service. These may be requested from:

> Superintendent of Documents
> U.S. Government Printing Office
> Washington, D.C. 20402

Publications of the state extension service. These publications are for local conditions, whereas the federal publications are generalized.

Publications of commercial plant, seed, and fertilizer companies.

National plant societies, such as the Geranium Society, the African Violet Society, the American Rock Garden Society, etc. The addresses of the forty or so national plant societies can be found in the American Horticultural Society's publication *Directory of American Horticulture*.

Associations

American Horticultural Society, Inc.
Mount Vernon
Virginia 22121

American Society for Horticultural Science
Atten. Cecil Blackwell
P.O. Box 109
St. Joseph, Michigan 49085

American Society of Landscape Architects
1750 Old Meadow Road
McLean, Virginia 22101

Garden Club of America
598 Madison Ave.
New York, New York 10022

Gardens For All, Inc.
The National Association For Gardening
Shelburne, Vermont 05482

Men's Garden Clubs of America
5560 Merle Way Road
Des Moines, Iowa 50323

National Council for Therapy and Rehabilitation Through Horticulture
Mount Vernon, Virginia 22121

The National Society of State Garden Clubs, Inc.
4401 Magnolia Ave.
St. Louis, Missouri 63110

Catalogues and Guides

American Gardens - A Traveler's Guide, $1.50
Brooklyn Botanic Garden
Brooklyn, New York 11225

Antaeus Books
Box 153, Granville, Massachusetts 01034. Will supply any book on gardening, farming, conservation, and ecology.

A Child's Garden, A Guide for Parents and Teachers
Chevron Chemical Company
P.O. Box 3744
San Francisco, California 94119

Directory of American Horticulture
American Horticultural Society
Mount Vernon, Virginia 22121

Guide to Community Garden Organization, $2.00
How to Start a School Gardening Program (Grades 4-6), $2.00
A Guide Through the Vegetable Garden, 1-10 - .50 ea., 11-50 - .45 ea., 51-100 -.40 ea., 101-500 - .35 ea., 501-up - .30 ea.
  All of the above available
  through Gardens for All, Inc.
  (address given under *Associations*)

National Agricultural Library
Beltsville, Maryland 21705
Will supply all nursery and seed trade catalogues.

Teachers' Guide to Minigardens
U.S. Department of Agriculture,
ARS, Information Division
Educational Services Branch
Agricultural Research Center
Beltsville, Maryland 20705

Yellow Pages—A Guide to Organized Environmental Efforts
Environmental Resources, Inc.
2000 P. St. N.W.,
Washington, D.C. 20036

Films

New Guidelines for the Well-Landscaped Home
A 14 minute USDA color film, available on loan from state film libraries, usually at state universities.

Growing, Growing
An 11 minute ecology film for kindergarten through third grade.
Available for preview or purchase from:
Churchill Films
622 N. Robertson Blvd.
Los Angeles, California 90069

Color it Green With Trees
50 frames, slide sets and filmstrips available, which show how to plant trees.
U.S. Department of Agriculture
Office of Information
Photo Library
Room 412A
Washington, D.C. 20250

Services available through the U.S. Department of Agriculture

Conservation of Natural Resources

Purpose: To help conservation districts and groups of farmers, ranchers, and other landowners conserve and improve natural resources.

How USDA can help: Soil Conservation Service (SCS) provides the services of professional conservationists to help plan and apply conservation measures. The Forest Service provides services on forestry matters through the state forestry agencies. Through pooling agreements between the Agricultural Stabilization and Conservation Service (ASCS) and community groups, costs are shared on community projects essential to natural resource conservation.

Who may apply: Any group of farmers, ranchers, or landowners in a community. Any individual farmer, rancher, or landowner may also apply to SCS for technical assistance and to ASCS for cost-sharing.

Where to apply: Local SCS and ASCS offices, usually located in the county seat.

Resource Conservation and Development Projects

Purpose: To stimulate economic growth in multi-county areas through accelerated conservation activities and land-use adjustments.

How USDA can help: Federal participation includes technical assistance to develop physically sound and economically justified long-range development plans; technical assistance to help landowners install needed conservation measures; cost-sharing assistance to public bodies on certain approved conservation and development measures having community benefits; and credit to help landowners and local sponsors finance planned capital improvements of soil and water resources.

Farmers Home Administration can make loans to public agencies and private non-profit corporations to provide for natural resource conservation and development in designated project areas, including outdoor recreation facilities.

Who may apply: Any legally qualified local group, such as a conservation district, local governing body, town, local or state agency, or public development corporation.

Where to apply: State Conservationist, Soil Conservation Service, or write to:
Administrator
Soil Conservation Service
U.S. Department of Agriculture

Washington, D.C. 20250

Purpose: To provide the area-wide planning needed to improve and effectively use existing resources for economic expansion.

How USDA can help: Agricultural Research Service gives direct assistance to communities and other groups in planning complete project proposals in the field of agribusiness, in evaluating projects at request of funding agencies, and in establishment and operation of agribusiness facilities. ARS and the Cooperative Extension Service also help local communities plan marketing facilities, such as wholesale food distribution centers, farmers markets, pack sheds, terminal markets, and livestock auction markets.

Soils and Land-Use Planning

Purpose: To provide soils and other information needed by rural and suburban communities to guide their changes in land use.

How USDA can help: Soil surveys and soil maps developed by SCS to determine community location of future recreation areas, airports, schools, etc.

Who may apply: Any public or private organization or individual.

Where to apply: State or local offices or the Soil Conservation Service or Forest Service or write to Administrator
                     Soil Conservation Service
                     or Chief, Forest Service
                     U.S. Department of Agriculture
                     Washington, D.C. 20250

Programs to Strengthen Cooperatives

Purpose: To help farmers and others in rural areas increase their income by improving the effectiveness of established and emerging cooperatives and to form new cooperatives to market, purchase, and obtain other services.

How USDA can help: Upon request, Farmer Cooperative Service works with cooperatives in defining and solving organization, operating, and management problems. It provides published material on all phases of cooperative operations.

Who may apply: Cooperative officials and community groups interested in developing cooperatives.

Where to apply:
     Administrator
     Farmer Cooperative Service
     U.S. Department of Agriculture
     Washington, D.C. 20250   **143**

Bibliography

ARTICLES:

Beatty, V.L. "Highrise Horticulture," *American Horticulturist,* 53 (2), Summer, 1974, 42-46.

Berry, J. "She Brings Nature to the City," *National Wildlife,* 14, October 1976, 6-7.

Cotton, M. "Horticultural Therapy," *Horticulture,* 53, September 1975, 24.

Grotzke, H. "What Biodynamics is All About," *Organic Gardening and Farming,* June 1975, 58-61.

Gaylin, J. "Green-Thumb Therapy For the Handicapped," *Psychology Today,* 9, April 1976, 118.

Horsbrugh, P., "Human-Plant Proximities: A Psychological Imperative," *Indiana Nursery News,* 33 (4) April 1972.

"Hortitherapy", *Science Digest,* 80, October 1976, 10.

Iltis, H., "Flowers and Human Ecology," *New Movements in the Study and Teaching of Biology,* Selmes, C. (ed.), Maurice Temple Smith, London, 289-317.

Iltis, H., Loucks, O.L., and Andrews, P., "Criteria for an Optimum Human Environment," *Bulletin of the Atomic Scientists,* 26 (1), 2-6.

Kaplan, R. "Some Psychological Benefits of Gardening," *Environment and Behavior,* 5 (2), June, 1973, 145-161.

Leon, C. "The Healing Power of Gardening," *House and Garden,* 148, February 1976, 134.

Lewis, C.A., "People-Plant Interaction: A Man-Environment Relationship," *Arboretum Bulletin,* XXXIX (1), Winter, 1976, 2-10.

Lewis, C.A., "People-Plant Interaction: A Man-Environment Relationship," *University of Washington Arboretum Bulletin,* XXXIX (1), Winter, 1976, 2-10.

Lewis, C.A., "Public Housing Gardens - Landscapes for the Soul," *Landscapes For Living,* USDA Yearbook of Agriculture, 1972, 277-282.

Lieberman, M. "Parks and Urban Mental Health," *Park Practice Trends,* 7 (3), 30-32.

Mann, P. "Miracle of the Flower Boxes," *The Reader's Digest,* 103, July 1973, 106-110.

Menninger, R. "Community Gardening," *The CoEvolution Quarterly,* Fall 1976, 72 & 73.

Moncrief, L.W., and Langsenkamp, R., "Cultivating Community Gardening," *Parks and Recreation,* 11, April, 1976, 19-21.

Nilsson, R. "The Big Organic Farm and the Man Who Made It Work," *Organic Gardening and Farming,* 19 (11) November 1972, 46.

Stainbrook, E., "Man's Psychic Need For Nature", *Parks and Conservation,* September, 1973, 22-23.

BOOKS:

Agriculture In The City, Santa Barbara, Calif,: Community Environmental Council, Inc., 1976.

Bush-Brown, L., *Garden Blocks for Urban America,* New York: Scribners, 1969.

Drake, S.Y., and Lawrence, R.L., *Recreational Community Gardening,* Washington, D.C.: U.S. Department of Interior, Bureau of Outdoor Recreation, 1976.

Dumont, M.P., *The Absurd Healer,* New York: Viking, 1971.

Hertzberg, R., Vaughn, B. and Greene, J., *Putting Food By,* Brattleboro, Vt.: Stephen Greene Press, 1973.

Hunter, B.T., *Gardening Without Poisons,* Boston: Houghton Mifflin, 2nd ed., 1972.

Jeavons, J., *How To Grow More Vegetables Than You Ever Thought Possible on Less Land Than You Can Imagine,* Palo Alto, Calif.: Ecology Action of The Mid-peninsula, 1975.

Newcomb, D., *The Postage Stamp Garden Book,* Los Angeles: J.P. Tarcher, Inc., 1975.

Newman, O., *Defensible Space,* New York: Macmillan, 1972.

Olkowski, H. and W., *The City People's Book of Raising Food,* Emmaus, Pa.: Rodale Press, Inc., 1975.

Pendergast, C., *Introduction to Organic Gardening,* Los Angeles: Nash Publishing, 1971.

Smith, W.G., *Gardening For Food,* New York: Scribners, 1972.

Solecki, R.S., *Shanidar: The First Flower People,* New York: Knopf, 1971.

Thurber, N. & Mead, G., *Keeping the Harvest,* Charlotte, Vt.: Garden Way, 1976.

Weil, A., *The Natural Mind,* Boston: Houghton Mifflin Co., 1973.

Widrig, R.S., *Sea Breezes and Vegetable Gardening,* Nova Scotia, Canada: Kentville Publishing Co., Ltd., 1967.

Index

8405